P9-ARY-100

New Directions for
Higher Education

Betsy Barefoot
EDITOR-IN-CHIEF

Dual Enrollment: Strategies, Outcomes, and Lessons for School–College Partnerships

Eric Hofmann
Daniel Voloch
EDITORS

Number 158 • Summer 2012
Jossey-Bass
San Francisco

Dual Enrollment: Strategies, Outcomes, and Lessons for School–College Partnerships
Eric Hofmann, Daniel Voloch
New Directions for Higher Education, no. 158
Betsy Barefoot, Editor-in-Chief

Microfilm copies of issues and articles are available in 16mm and 35mm, as well as microfiche in 105mm, through University Microfilms Inc., 300 North Zeeb Road, Ann Arbor, MI 48106-1346.

NEW DIRECTIONS FOR HIGHER EDUCATION (ISSN 0271-0560, electronic ISSN 1536-0741) is part of The Jossey-Bass Higher and Adult Education Series and is published quarterly by Wiley Subscription Services, Inc., A Wiley Company, at Jossey-Bass, One Montgomery Street, Suite 1200, San Francisco, CA 94104-4594. Periodicals Postage Paid at San Francisco, California, and at additional mailing offices. POSTMASTER: Send address changes to New Directions for Higher Education, Jossey-Bass, One Montgomery Street, Suite 1200, San Francisco, CA 94104-4594.

New Directions for Higher Education is indexed in Current Index to Journals in Education (ERIC); Higher Education Abstracts.

SUBSCRIPTIONS cost $89 for individuals and $275 for institutions, agencies, and libraries. See ordering information page at end of journal.

EDITORIAL CORRESPONDENCE should be sent to the Editor-in-Chief, Betsy Barefoot, Gardner Institute, Box 72, Brevard, NC 28712.

Cover photograph © Digital Vision

www.josseybass.com

CONTENTS

1

Providing an overview of the volume, this chapter summarizes the evolution of dual enrollment programs over the past decade and discusses the role dual enrollment can play in the nation's college-completion agenda.

Why Dual Enrollment?

Eric Hofmann

This volume focuses on the designs and goals, policies and practices, and short- and long-term outcomes of programs that enroll high school students in college courses for college credit. Commonly referred to as "dual enrollment" programs—participants are enrolled at both the high school and college—these programs belong to a broader category commonly referred to as "college transition programs" (U.S. Department of Education 2003a). Dual enrollment and its counterparts, such as "dual credit" and "concurrent enrollment," are known as "credit-based transition programs" (Bailey and Karp 2003), a category that includes International Baccalaureate programs (IB), Advanced Placement (AP), and early college high schools.

In 2005, the U.S. Department of Education published statistics on dual enrollment participation based on a national survey (Kleiner and Lewis 2005). In their review of postsecondary institutions offering dual enrollment opportunities, the survey authors defined college course-taking either (1) as part of a program, which is "an organized system with special guidelines that allows high school students to take college-level courses" (Kleiner and Lewis 2005, 1), or (2) as an individual high school student enrolling on her own in a college course. The survey found that, in 2002–2003, 57 percent of all Title IV degree-granting institutions offered dual enrollment within or outside of a structured program. At that time, 98 percent of public two-year institutions offered some form of dual enrollment, compared to 77 percent of public four-year institutions. The survey also indicated that 40 percent of private four-year institutions and 17 percent of private two-year institutions offered courses for college credit to high school students. Overall, the authors estimated that 813,000 high school students took a college-level course during that time. As of this writing, a new study of the national scope of dual enrollment is underway, with an expected publication date of summer 2012 (Personal communication with Stephanie Marken of Westat, December 2011).

New Directions for Higher Education, no. 158, Summer 2012 © Wiley Periodicals, Inc.
Published online in Wiley Online Library (wileyonlinelibrary.com) • DOI:10.1002/he.20009

Much has happened in the world of dual enrollment since 2002–2003. More states have added policies to govern program implementation, the school reform and standards debate has escalated, and college completion has become the dominant topic in a national conversation around the position of the United States in the global economy. The authors included in this volume represent a variety of perspectives on dual enrollment and the broader theme of preparing high school students for postsecondary success. They include researchers who have investigated various aspects of dual enrollment for the better part of the last decade and administrators who oversee local programs. Collectively, their work in this volume demonstrates the opportunities and long-term possibilities that come from linking high school and college more intentionally so that students are better prepared to confront the academic, social, and financial challenges that await them after high school.

The College Completion Agenda

In fall 2003 under the framework of No Child Left Behind, the U.S. Department of Education held a one-day summit and published a series of issue papers intended to promote a dialogue on the topic of school transformation (U.S. Department of Education 2003c). One primary theme addressed at the conference was accelerating high school students' transition into work or additional education; the initiative urged high schools to "work with higher education and the business community to define the necessary knowledge and skills for success after high school, to make sure students know what those requirements are, and to give students every opportunity to acquire them" (http://www2.ed.gov/about/offices/list/ovae/pi/hsinit/trans.html).

Conversations around higher education have focused recently on both the beginning and endpoint of college: the number of students entering in need of remediation and the stagnant—if not declining—completion rates. For example, President Obama's call to increase college graduation rates by 2020 was the foundation of the American Graduation Initiative he proposed in 2009. Delivering his speech in suburban Detroit, the president made a significant gesture when he spotlighted the role community colleges would play in the nation's economic recovery. Although funding for the full initiative never materialized, conversations about college readiness and completion have escalated, as seen through the likes of the American Diploma Project on the one end, which seeks to strengthen the rigor of high school courses, and Achieving the Dream on the other, which focuses on student success in community colleges. Dual enrollment bridges these initiatives.

Of course, low rates of degree completion are not only a community college issue. For example, of all the students who graduated from Chicago Public Schools in 1998 or 1999 and entered a four-year college immediately after graduation, only 35 percent earned a bachelor's degree within six years

(Roderick 2006). A study by the National Center for Education Statistics (Berkner et al. 2002, iv) reinforces the dilemma: "Among all beginners at 4-year institutions in 1995–96, 51 percent completed a bachelor's degree within 6 years at the first institution attended." Accounting for transfer, the rate was 58 percent. And for recent high school graduates and also accounting for transfer, it was 64 percent. By comparison, of the community college students who indicated an intention to earn some postsecondary degree (75 percent of all students in the study), 31 percent earned either an associate's or a bachelor's degree after six years.

Strategies that can contribute to both goals—that is, better preparation and therefore higher college completion rates—begin in high school. Dual enrollment embodies the college transition agenda from its unique position in the middle space—or gap—between high school achievement and college readiness. Implemented for several decades by individual institutions across the country to introduce high academic achievers to local higher education opportunities, dual enrollment today has taken on several goals, one of which is to provide access and support for students traditionally at risk of educational failure. The 2005 study estimated that 5 percent of the 2,050 institutions nationally that offered structured dual enrollment programs served this population (Kleiner and Lewis 2005); the recent survey covering the 2010–2011 academic year includes a series of questions focused specifically on whether there has been growth in programming to serve these students.

Dual enrollment fits into the larger framework of college readiness as described by Conley (2005, 2007, 2010). In a recent study funded by MDRC, Rutschow and Schneider (2011) highlight dual enrollment as a promising strategy with regard to remedial education. And with respect to completion, Adelman (2004, 2006) and Swanson (2008) have described the potential benefit of earning college credit prior to matriculating as a regularly enrolled college student. However, although research on dual enrollment has generally been positive, the body of work is not exhaustive. Much of it comes from a few sources: the Community College Research Center at Teachers College, Columbia University, and Jobs for the Future, a nonprofit education and workforce development organization in Boston. Allen (2010) provides a comprehensive literature review of the subject, including experimental studies that show correlation between dual enrollment and postsecondary success.

On the whole, researchers agree dual enrollment would benefit from deeper investigation (Bailey and Morest 2006; Rutschow and Schneider 2011). These sentiments echo a call by the Office of Vocational and Adult Education (U.S. Department of Education 2003b, 2) dating back to the earlier conversations at the U. S. Department of Education for more research on dual enrollment: "While dual enrollment programs have the potential to help students enter and succeed in postsecondary education, there are many factors that still need to be explored. More information is needed on:

1. How many and what types of students participate in dual enrollment;
2. What program features are most common;
3. Whether these efforts support the transition and persistence of students in postsecondary education; and
4. How state policies influence program structures and practices.

With these questions in mind, this volume is intended to serve both as a resource for those interested in dual enrollment and as a forum for fostering further conversations about these programs.

Policy and Program Practices

The American Youth Policy Forum, a nonprofit professional development organization based in Washington, DC, has been documenting state policies around dual enrollment for many years and hosted a forum on dual enrollment in 2005 (http://www.aypf.org/forumbriefs/2005/fb102805.htm). Recent figures concerning the policies and funding structures for dual enrollment (Barnett and Stamm 2010) indicate that forty-six states have policies governing these programs, with twelve states making participation mandatory for public higher education institutions. It is the role of postsecondary institutions and local school districts to determine how to enact these policies for high school participants.

Dual enrollment comes in many shapes and sizes, but at its foundation is college course-taking. Some programs invite students to the campus to enroll in a course populated with matriculated college students; others combine students from several high schools into one classroom on the campus. In order to provide the widest access to dual enrollment, many programs have high school students participate in college-credit courses that are offered at the high school and taught by a high school instructor who is appointed as a college adjunct. This latter model is common to programs that have been accredited by the National Alliance for Concurrent Enrollment Programs (NACEP), a professional organization with 180 postsecondary members and 41 high schools and school districts. As of fall 2010, thirty-one public two-year colleges, twenty-one public four-year universities, and five private four-year colleges and universities had been accredited according to the organization's standards (http://nacep.org/about/mission-and-history/). A distinguishing feature of NACEP (2011) is that member organizations offer college courses during the school day.

In his keynote address at the NACEP 2011 national gathering hosted by the University of Connecticut, David Conley emphasized the important role dual enrollment plays in helping students become college and career ready. His presentation highlighted salient issues for program administrators, such as scalability and quality control. These and a host of other issues are the focus of the diverse chapters included here.

How We Have Organized the Volume

In this sourcebook, researchers and practitioners discuss the impact of dual enrollment programs on student achievement, institutional practice, and the role of higher education in improving K–12. We have divided Chapters Two through Ten into two sections. The chapters in the first section explore dual enrollment from a variety of angles. To begin, Allen and Dadgar in Chapter Two illustrate the results of the most rigorous study of dual enrollment to date and suggest a potential causal relationship between dual enrollment participation and postsecondary performance. Chapters Three and Four illustrate how dual enrollment effects important transformations in student participants and college instructors. For example, Karp posits that students in dual enrollment participate in anticipatory socialization and are able to learn the role of the college student in advance of matriculation. Meanwhile, Hughes and Edwards demonstrate how the dual enrollment classroom is improving pedagogy and curriculum in California institutions. Their findings are consonant with the curriculum and instruction goals of Achieving the Dream, the national nonprofit organization whose primary goal is to help community college students complete a degree.

In Chapters Five and Six, administrators of two programs—one for honors students, the other focusing primarily on high school students in the academic midrange—demonstrate how the definitions of success for dual enrollment might change depending on the program goals and how they are measured. First, Kinnick highlights the impact of the Kennesaw State University Dual Enrollment Honors Program on this Georgia institution. Next, Kim describes dual enrollment across New York City, illustrating how an intentional and thoughtful use of data reveals that meeting certain program management priorities might mask problems in other areas.

The final chapter of the first section, Chapter Seven, observes dual enrollment alongside another popular college-level transition program: Advanced Placement (AP). Using Texas data, Klopfenstein and Lively suggest that dual enrollment and AP might better serve different populations, highlighting the value of providing different pathways. As indicated in some of the preceding chapters, the authors' suggestion that there are several different college preparatory pathways resonates with the idea of "matching"—helping students make the most rigorous selection based on their capabilities, as described by Roderick et al. (2008) and Bowen, Chingas, and McPherson (2009) in reference to the college application process.

The second section of the volume explores models that build upon the foundation of dual enrollment with the goal of strengthening school–college partnerships. The initiatives described in these chapters embrace a more robust framework for supporting college transition than a program design based primarily on a single course, sometimes referred to as the "singleton" model (Bailey and Karp 2003). Venezia and Voloch in Chapter Eight introduce programs intended to support high school seniors who are on track to graduate but have not met the benchmarks for remediation exemption in two state systems: the California State University (CSU) system of four-year colleges and The City University of New York (CUNY). For CUNY, this means taking the remedial activities that had been offered through dual enrollment and incorporating them into the school day. Other states are pursuing similar work. For example, the Southern Regional Education Board is reviewing the progress of six states in its region that are implementing senior-year transition courses in math and English. The organization's Website provides resources that will help schools align senior-year curriculum with college and career readiness.

In Chapter Nine, Edmunds shares initial lessons learned from North Carolina's extensive experiment with early college high schools. These schools are not only changing the trajectory of traditionally underrepresented populations, they are also influencing conversations around the importance of partnerships between K–12 and higher education.

Dual Enrollment and New York City

Chapters Two, Three, Six, Eight, and Ten reference programs in CUNY, a system whose seventeen undergraduate campuses run a coordinated dual enrollment program referred to collectively as College Now. College Now links the country's largest urban education systems, and this unique partnership between the New York City Department of Education and CUNY has provided a rich environment for experimentation and research. In recent months, educational administrators in the state of Massachusetts, from the city of Chicago system, and even at private institutions such as Ohio Dominican University and Duke University, have reached out to CUNY for input on dual enrollment implementation. Education being local, however, it is impossible to single out any one program for replication in another context, as CUNY practitioners have learned in the past eleven years.

Considering that New York State is one of only a handful of states that does not have a dual enrollment policy, CUNY programs are afforded great flexibility yet warrant genuine uncertainty with regard to program implementation and funding. Even so, as indicated by CUNY's executive vice chancellor and university provost (Logue 2010), a "system approach" to higher education provides a space for experimentation and the possibility of scaling successful practices. With this in mind, Chapter Ten describes how the insights of dual enrollment administrators and faculty provided an understanding of the obstacles faced by the typical community college student and contributed to plans for The New Community College at CUNY. Meade highlights how the lessons learned from implementing a systemwide approach to dual enrollment helped inform several aspects of the model, from the design of the first-year program to the use of data to inform academic and student services in order to build the university's first new college in 40 years.

Conclusion

Geography, institutional desire and capacity, policy: All play important and often competing roles in this work. It is difficult to know what pieces are missing in college readiness if postsecondary institutions are not engaged with students—and schools—before matriculation. In the final chapter of the volume, Chapter Eleven, we tackle some of the tensions inherent in the field of dual enrollment, from the role of K–12 education in the college or university mission to questions of what happens in a college classroom. We suggest that the space inhabited by dual enrollment is useful for addressing larger issues of postsecondary practice.

References

Adelman, C. 2004. *Principal Indicators of Student Academic Histories in Postsecondary Education, 1972–2000*. Washington, DC: U.S. Department of Education, Institute of Education Sciences.

Adelman, C. 2006. *The Toolbox Revisited: Paths to Degree Completion From High School Through College*. Washington, DC: U.S. Department of Education, Office of Vocational and Adult Education.

Allen, D. 2010. *Dual Enrollment: A Comprehensive Literature Review and Bibliography*. New York: City University of New York. Accessed September 1, 2011, from http://www.cuny.edu/academics/k-to-12/databook/library/DE_LitReview_August2010.pdf.

Bailey, T., and M. M. Karp. 2003. "Promoting College Access and Success: A Review of Credit-Based Transition Programs." Washington, DC: Office of Vocational and Adult Education, U.S. Department of Education.

Bailey, T., and V. S. Morest. 2006. "The Community College Equity Agenda in the Twenty-First Century: Moving from Access to Achievement." In *Defending the Community College Agenda*, edited by T. Bailey and V. S. Morest. Baltimore: Johns Hopkins University Press.

Barnett, E., and L. Stamm. 2010. *Dual Enrollment: A Strategy for Educational Advancement of All Students*. Washington, DC: Blackboard Institute.

Berkner, L., S. He, E. F. Cataldi, and P. Knepper. 2002. *Descriptive Summary of 1995–1996 Beginning Postsecondary Students: Six Years Later*. Washington, DC: National Center for Education Statistics.

Bowen, W. G., M. M. Chingas, and M. S. McPherson. 2009. *Crossing the Finish Line: Completing College at America's Public Universities*. Princeton, NJ: Princeton University Press.

Conley, D. 2005. *College Knowledge*. San Francisco: Jossey-Bass.

Conley, D. 2007. *Redefining College Readiness, Volume 3*. Eugene, OR: Educational Policy Improvement Center.

Conley, D. 2010. *College and Career Ready*. San Francisco: Jossey-Bass.

Conley, D. 2011. "The Continuum of College and Career Readiness: Creating Successful Transitions to Postsecondary Education." Paper presented at NACEP National Conference, Mystic, Connecticut, October.

Kleiner, B., and L. Lewis. 2005. *Dual Enrollment of High School Students at Postsecondary Institutions: 2002–03*. Washington, DC: National Center for Education Statistics, U.S. Department of Education.

Logue, A. 2010. "The Power of the System." Accessed December 1, 2011, from http://www.insidehighered.com/views/2010/05/21/logue.

National Alliance of Concurrent Enrollment Programs (NACEP). 2011. "Standards." Accessed November 10, 2011, from http://nacep.org/standards/.

Roderick, M. 2006. *Closing the Aspirations-Attainment Gap: Implications for High School Reform: A Commentary from Chicago.* New York: MDRC.

Roderick, M., J. Nagaoka, V. Coca, and E. Moeller. 2008. *From High School to the Future: Potholes on the Road to College.* Chicago: Consortium on Chicago School Research at the University of Chicago.

Rutschow, E. Z., and E. Schneider. 2011. *Unlocking the Gate: What We Know About Improving Developmental Education.* New York: MDRC.

Swanson, J. 2008. "An Analysis of the Impact of High School Dual Enrollment Course Participation on Post-Secondary Academic Success, Persistence and Degree Completion." Iowa City: Institute for Research and Policy Acceleration at the Belin-Blank Center for Gifted Education, University of Iowa.

U.S. Department of Education. (2003a). *College Transition Programs: Promoting Success Beyond High School.* The High School Leadership Summit Issues Paper. Washington, DC: Office of Vocational and Adult Education, U.S. Department of Education.

U.S. Department of Education. (2003b). *Dual Enrollment: Accelerating the Transition to College.* The High School Leadership Summit Issues Paper. Washington, DC: Office of Vocational and Adult Education, U.S. Department of Education.

U.S. Department of Education. (2003c). "Preparing America's Future High School Initiative." Accessed December 1, 2011, from http://www2.ed.gov/about/offices/list/ovae/pi/hsinit/index.html.

ERIC HOFMANN *is university director for Collaborative Programs at The City University of New York.*

Section I. Various Perspectives on Dual Enrollment

2

This chapter reviews previous studies on dual enrollment and discusses the results of an evaluation of College Now, the dual enrollment program of The City University of New York. The authors find that dual enrollment participation increases postsecondary achievement.

Does Dual Enrollment Increase Students' Success in College? Evidence from a Quasi-Experimental Analysis of Dual Enrollment in New York City

Drew Allen, Mina Dadgar

This chapter discusses new evidence on the effectiveness of dual enrollment in increasing college achievement in New York City (NYC). After reviewing existing research on the effectiveness of dual enrollment programs, we discuss the results of a recent evaluation of College Now, the dual enrollment program of The City University of New York (CUNY). We find that enrolling in a College Now dual enrollment course reduces time to degree, not only by allowing students to earn college credits before entering college but also by increasing the number of college courses students take once they are enrolled in college. Furthermore, we find that the program also increases students' academic performance as measured by higher college grade point average (GPA). Our study affirms the findings from recent quantitative evaluations of dual enrollment that the programs can indeed help improve postsecondary attainment and reduce time to degree.

What Do We Know about the Effectiveness of Dual Enrollment?

Previous studies of dual enrollment have been predominantly qualitative in nature or based on single institution samples. Bailey and Karp (2003) and Lerner and Brand (2006) provide extensive reviews of this literature. However, with improvements in data quality in recent years, more rigorous quantitative evaluations of dual enrollment programs have emerged. The most rigorous studies have found that dual enrollment increases postsecondary

New Directions for Higher Education, no. 158, Summer 2012 © Wiley Periodicals, Inc.
Published online in Wiley Online Library (wileyonlinelibrary.com) • DOI:10.1002/he.20010

enrollment and success (Allen 2010). These studies include evaluations of dual enrollment programs in Florida (Karp et al. 2007; Speroni 2010) and in New York City (Karp et al. 2007), as well as a study based on a nationally representative sample (Swanson 2008). These three studies are particularly rigorous because they are based on large representative datasets and, at a minimum, are able to control for some measure of preprogram academic achievement when comparing outcomes of program participants and nonparticipants. Although these studies focus on different samples of students and use different statistical models, they all find positive outcomes for students who participated in dual enrollment.

Karp et al. (2007) examined the effect of participation in dual enrollment programs for students who were in career and technical education (CTE) high school programs in New York City, and for both CTE and non-CTE students in Florida. When comparing outcomes for students who participated in dual enrollment and those who did not, the authors control for differences in race, gender, socioeconomic status (SES), high school GPA, grade level, and school demographics. The authors found positive effects across several indicators of success for both CTE and non-CTE students. For example, in both Florida and NYC, participation in dual enrollment was positively related to enrollment in college, persistence to the second semester, higher GPA, and attainment of more credits within three years of high school graduation for both the full sample and for the CTE students.

Swanson (2008) used the nationally representative sample (National Education Longitudinal Study:88/00) and found that dual enrollment increased college persistence after accounting for some of the preexisting differences among participants and nonparticipants, including gender, race, first-generation college enrollment, SES, high school GPA, and class rank. Both of these aforementioned studies control for several of the preexisting differences between program participants and the comparison group; however, to the extent that the controls do not capture unobserved differences among students such as motivation or resilience, the results may contain some bias.

In order to overcome such potential bias, Speroni (2010) used a particularly rigorous statistical methodology—regression discontinuity design—to compare program participants in Florida to statistically identical nonparticipants in terms of both observable and unobservable student characteristics such as motivation. She found very large positive effects for program participants who enrolled in a popular math course, College Algebra. Although this study uses a method that dramatically improves the methods used in previous literature, it has one possible shortcoming in that it relies on the sample of students who scored close to the eligibility cutoff for the program (high school GPA of 3.0 in the case of Florida); thus, the results may or may not be valid for students who had much higher or much lower academic achievements. Another potential limitation of this strategy is that it reduces the sample size to a very small number of students, which makes it difficult or impossible to detect effects that are moderate in magnitude.

Our study builds on the previous literature and attempts in several ways to advance what we currently know about the effectiveness of dual enrollment:

We attempt to account for the differences in demographic characteristics and preexisting academic differences between program participants and nonparticipants by controlling for an exceptionally rich set of demographic and academic achievement indicators.

We address the concern that there may be unobserved preexisting differences between program participants and nonparticipants by using a separate statistical strategy (difference in differences strategy) that attempts to account for both observable and unobservable differences among program participants and the comparison group.

We use a very large sample of students and may therefore be able to estimate program effects more precisely.

Dual Enrollment in New York City

The City University of New York's College Now program is the nation's largest dual enrollment initiative in an urban public school setting. The program, like many dual enrollment programs across the United States, offers high school students the opportunity to enroll in college courses and earn college credit while still in high school. Even though the College Now program models at each of the seventeen CUNY campuses incorporate varying course structures, locations, instructor affiliations, and so on, the programs are all similar in terms of overall administrative structure and goals (see Kim in Chapter Six of this volume). The program's stated goals are to improve graduation rates of NYC public school students, increase their level of preparation for college, and enable greater success in college. College Now is considered a comprehensive dual enrollment program because, in addition to college credit courses, it also offers students opportunities to enroll in zero-credit college preparation courses and workshops that aim to prepare students for college-level work. To allow for easier generalization of our findings to similar dual enrollment programs, this study focuses on the effects of the college-credit courses, and we identify program participants as students who completed at least one credit-bearing course.

Study Methodology. This study attempts to address the following question: What is the impact of dual enrollment on students' college credit accumulation, GPA, and retention? We make use of existing administrative data on CUNY's College Now program to address these questions. Our sample includes first-time freshmen who entered one of the seventeen CUNY colleges in the fall of 2009 and who had enrolled within fifteen months of graduating from a NYC public high school (n = 22,962). Student-level academic and demographic data for public high school students were obtained from the NYC Department of Education and were merged with data extracts from CUNY's Institutional Research Database and College Now program databases. This resulted in a linked dataset that includes records for every NYC public high school graduate who subsequently enrolled in a CUNY college, which represents approximately two-thirds of all matriculating college students from NYC public schools.

A limitation of our sample is that it includes only students who attend a CUNY college. Although we are able to track students' enrollment into colleges outside of the CUNY system through the National Student Clearinghouse, we do not have information about credits earned, GPA, and persistence for these students. Therefore, to the extent that the effect of the program is different for students who do not attend CUNY colleges, the results may not be generalizable to them.

We examine the effect of participation in dual enrollment on college success using three different outcomes: the number of credits earned during the first semester of college (excluding dual enrollment credits), first semester GPA, and CUNY systemwide retention to a third semester. We first estimate results based on comparing outcomes of CUNY first-time freshmen who completed at least one College Now credit course from any CUNY campus with a course outcome other than "official withdrawal" with outcomes of those public school graduates who never enrolled in a College Now credit course. We accounted for all observable differences among the students (regression adjusted estimates). This analysis uses a particularly rich set of demographic and prior achievement controls, including the following: race, gender, age, and indicators for free or reduced-price lunch status and language minority status; New York State Regents Exam scores for English Language Arts (ELA), mathematics, and global history; New York State eighth-grade English and math test scores; and verbal and math SAT scores. We also include high school fixed effects, which take into account institutional differences among schools. This allows us to address statistically the possible nonrandom matching of students across schools.

Table 2.1 compares demographic characteristics and preprogram participation exam scores for students who completed a College Now credit course and for students who did not. It is clear from the descriptive comparisons of background characteristics and preprogram achievement scores that students who participate in College Now have relatively higher academic achievement. This is considered positive selection of program participants in this type of analysis, and so failing to control fully for preexisting differences could result in overestimating the program effect. In this study, we not only control for demographic characteristics and several measures of academic achievement, but we also attempt to account for any unobserved preexisting differences between program participants and the comparison group by employing the quasi-experimental difference in differences analysis.

NEW DIRECTIONS FOR HIGHER EDUCATION • DOI:10.1002/he

**Table 2.1. Demographic Characteristics and Preprogram Exam
Scores by Program Participation**

	Demographic Characteristics	
	Nonparticipant	*Participant*
Asian	19%	26%
Black	28%	24%
Hispanic	38%	27%
White	15%	23%
Female	53%	62%
Free or Reduced-Price Lunch	50%	51%
Born in the United States	64%	61%
Native Language is English	60%	55%

	Exam Scores	
	Nonparticipant	*Participant*
SAT Verbal Score (mean)	425	453
SAT Math Score (mean)	450	477
8th-Grade ELA Score (mean)	694	700
8th-Grade Math Score (mean)	718	725
First ELA Regents Score (mean)	71	79
First Math Regents Score (mean)	72	77

Source: Authors' calculations using CUNY's Institutional Research Database, CUNY's College Now Database, and the New York City Department of Education.

Notes: Sample includes 22,962 first-time freshmen entering CUNY in fall of 2009 who had graduated from a NYC public high school within fifteen months of enrollment in CUNY and who pursued a (noncertificate) credential.

Findings. The results (Table 2.2) suggest that completing one or more College Now dual enrollment courses is associated with positive and substantial gains including earning more credits during the first semester of college and a higher college GPA. The regression results suggest that positive and significant effects hold after controlling for a rich set of students' demographic characteristics, high school grades, test performance, and the high school they attended. Of the three models employed in this analysis, our preferred regression model (3)—which includes all demographic and achievement controls as well as high school fixed effects—demonstrates that taking one or more College Now credit-bearing class is associated with almost one additional credit earned during the first semester, 0.16 points higher GPA in the first semester, and 5 percentage points greater likelihood of reenrolling in the third semester.

Difference in Differences. As mentioned previously, we are concerned that these results could be driven by unobserved differences among program participants and nonparticipants that are not captured by our demographic controls and measures of academic achievement. In order to test if this is

Table 2.2. Regression Adjusted Relationship between Taking a College Now Dual Enrollment Course and Academic Outcomes

Outcomes	Credits Earned			GPA			Retention to Subsequent Semester		
Model	(1)	(2)	(3)	(1)	(2)	(3)	(1)	(2)	(3)
College Now	2.095***	1.013***	0.925***	0.296***	0.151***	0.164***	0.086***	0.050***	0.048***
	(0.148)	(0.0892)	(0.0763)	(0.0276)	(0.0217)	(0.0189)	(0.00840)	(0.00771)	(0.00756)
Includes Demographic Controls	X	X	X	X	X	X	X	X	X
Includes Prior Achievement		X	X		X	X		X	X
Includes High School Fixed Effects			X			X			X
Observations	22,962	22,962	22,962	21,683	21,683	21,683	22,962	22,962	22,962
R-squared	0.148	0.368	0.391	0.085	0.184	0.216	0.054	0.092	0.121

Source: Authors' calculations using CUNY's Institutional Research Database, CUNY's Dual Enrollment Database, and the New York City Department of Education.

Notes: Sample includes 22,962 first-time freshmen entering CUNY in fall of 2009 who had graduated from a NYC public high school within fifteen months of enrollment in CUNY and who pursued a (noncertificate) credential. Model (1) includes a list of covariates including race; gender; an indicator for whether the native language is English, Spanish, or other; whether or not the student received free or reduced-price lunch while in high school; whether or not the student was born in the United States. In addition to these demographic characteristics, model (2) includes preprogram achievement measures including math and verbal SAT scores, first attempted Math and English Language Arts (ELA) Regents Exam scores, New York State eighth-grade math and English test scores, and indicators for missing values, as well as high school characteristics including enrollment size, school poverty, and school retention. Model (3) adds high school fixed effects to the previous measures. Robust standard errors are in parentheses. ***$p < 0.01$, **$p < 0.05$, *$p < 0.1$

the case, we compare our results from this regression analysis with the quasi-experimental results from a difference in differences (DID) approach. The DID strategy takes advantage of the fact that, although College Now has technically been available to every NYC public high school student, in reality, participation varies considerably by high school in often idiosyncratic ways. Some schools have high rates of College Now participation whereas others have very low rates or none. Using this variation in dual enrollment offering as well as program eligibility as determined by standardized exam scores, we employ a DID framework that compares eligible and ineligible students across schools that offer College Now and those that have little or no College Now participation.

In this method, we control for the same preexisting student characteristics and academic achievement indicators that were used in our initial regression analysis. Our first step is to calculate the difference in college outcomes (credit attainment, GPA, and retention) between eligible and ineligible students at schools that offer College Now. Next we compare that difference with the difference between eligible and ineligible students at schools that do not offer College Now. The effect of College Now can thus be considered the variation in the two differences—or the "difference in differences." This represents the effect of being an eligible student at a College Now partner school over and above the effect of being a student who is eligible for the program at any school and over and above the effect associated with attending a partner school. Employing this quasi-experimental strategy, which attempts to account for some of the unobserved differences among students, allows for causal interpretation of the effect of dual enrollment under certain assumptions, the primary one being that even if there are differences between College Now partner schools and nonpartner schools, the effect of being at a partner school is not different for eligible and ineligible students.

We find that our DID regression results (Table 2.3) are very similar to our initial regression results for two of the outcomes: the effects of the program on first-semester GPA and first-semester credits earned. However, in the quasi-experimental model, we are no longer able to detect any program effect for retention. Therefore, using this methodology, we are able to assert only that College Now increases credit attainment and improves college GPA. It should be noted that the effect sizes we find are considered to be large in the context of educational interventions; for example, the additional number of credits earned amounts to one-fifth of a standard deviation of additional college credits associated with program participation.

Conclusion

Our results confirm previous literature in that we also find large and positive effects of the program in helping students earn more credits even after

Table 2.3. Quasi-Experimental (DID) Estimates of the Effect of Taking a College Now Dual Enrollment Course and Being a College Now Eligible Student at a College Now "Partner" School

Outcomes	Credits Earned			GPA			Retention to Subsequent Semester		
Model	(1)	(2)	(3)	(1)	(2)	(3)	(1)	(2)	(3)
Participating in College Now	4.490***	1.295	1.617	1.027***	0.660	0.711*	0.245***	−0.226	−0.216
	(0.656)	(1.586)	(1.558)	(0.161)	(0.412)	(0.407)	(0.0630)	(0.162)	(0.159)
Includes Covariates	X	X	X	X	X	X	X	X	X
Includes Linear ELA Regent Scores	X		X	X		X	X		X
Includes High School Fixed Effects		X	X		X	X		X	X
Observations	22,962	22,962	22,962	21,683	21,683	21,683	22,962	22,962	22,962

Source: Authors' calculations using CUNY's Institutional Research Database, CUNY's Dual Enrollment Database, and the New York City Department of Education.

Notes: Sample includes 22,962 first-time freshmen entering CUNY in fall of 2009 who had graduated from a NYC public high school within fifteen months of enrollment in CUNY and who pursued a (noncertificate) credential. All models include the main effects of being eligible for College Now and Attending a College Now "Partner" School, and a list of covariates including race; gender; an indicator for whether the native language is English, Spanish, or other; whether or not the student received free or reduced-price lunch while in high school; whether or not the student was born in the United States, math and verbal SAT scores, first attempted Math (ELA) Regents Exam scores, New York State eighth-grade math and English exam scores, as well as indicators for missing values. In addition, models 1 and 3 include a linear measure of the ELA Regents Exam score, which is the most common indicator of eligibility. Models 2 and 3 include an indicator variable that specifies the students' high school of entry thus controlling for the general effect of a high school on all students (whether or not the students are eligible for the program). Robust standard errors are in parentheses. ***$p < 0.01$, **$p < 0.05$, *$p < 0.1$

they have enrolled in college and in earning higher grades in college. The similarities between our regression and our quasi-experimental results suggest that, when studies are able to control for measures of preprogram achievement, their results closely approximate more sophisticated analyses that account for some of the unobserved differences among students. In other words, using preprogram proxies for ability and achievements including state Regents scores, grades in the eighth grade, and SAT scores seems to capture the differences in students' ability, motivation, and preparation that lead to differences in college achievement. This can increase our confidence in the results found by Karp et al. (2007) and Swanson (2008).

As time to degree has increased in recent years, "academic momentum" has become an important issue in helping students graduate and to do so on time (Scott-Clayton 2011). These preliminary results suggest that College Now may help reduce time to degree not only by helping students earn college credits but also by increasing credit attainment even after students enter college.

References

Allen, D. 2010. *Dual Enrollment: A Comprehensive Literature and Bibliography*. New York: Office of Collaborative Programs, City University of New York.

Bailey, T. R., and M. M. Karp. 2003. *Promoting College Access and Success: A Review of Dual Credit and Other High School/College Transition Programs*. Washington, DC: U.S. Department of Education.

Karp, M. M., J. C. Calcagno, K. L. Hughes, D. W. Jeong, and T. R. Bailey. 2007. *The Postsecondary Achievement of Participants in Dual Enrollment: An Analysis of Student Outcomes in Two States*. St. Paul: National Research Center for Career and Technical Education, University of Minnesota.

Lerner, J. B., and B. Brand. 2006. *The College Ladder: Linking Secondary and Postsecondary Education for Success for All Students*. Washington, DC: American Youth Policy Forum.

Scott-Clayton, J. 2011. "The Rise of Five-Year Four-Year Degree." *New York Times*. May 20.

Speroni, C. 2010. *High School Dual Enrollment Programs: Are We Fast-Tracking Students Too Fast?* Job Market Paper. New York: Teachers College, Columbia University.

Swanson, J. 2008. "An Analysis of the Impact of High School Dual Enrollment Course Participation on Post-Secondary Academic Success, Persistence and Degree Completion." Iowa City: Institute for Research and Policy Acceleration at the Belin-Blank Center for Gifted Education, University of Iowa.

DREW ALLEN *is director of research and evaluation for Collaborative Programs at The City University of New York.*

MINA DADGAR *is a doctoral candidate in economics and education at Columbia University's Teachers College and research associate at the Community College Research Center.*

NEW DIRECTIONS FOR HIGHER EDUCATION • DOI:10.1002/he

This chapter provides a theoretical framework through which to understand the experiences of dual enrollment students. Through anticipatory socialization and role rehearsal, participants "try out" the role of college student and develop the skills necessary for future postsecondary success.

3

"I don't know, I've never been to college!" Dual Enrollment as a College Readiness Strategy

Melinda Mechur Karp

As referenced in Chapters One and Two of this volume, there is some evidence that positive academic outcomes in high school and college are related to dual enrollment participation for middle- and even low-achieving students. But the reality is that most dual enrollment programs are intended for students with at least some basic level of college academic skills, as they require students to meet entry or college-readiness standards (Hughes et al. 2005; Kleiner and Lewis 2005; Waits, Setzer, and Lewis 2005). Given this reality, should we really view dual enrollment as an intervention that boosts students' academic skills? Why work to improve the academic proficiency of students who are already, at least by some measures, proficient?

There is a more compelling explanation for the importance and potential of dual enrollment. Creating an overarching framework that explains why dual enrollment programs can contribute to college preparation, broadly defined, can help focus our expectations and articulate to policymakers why this intervention is an important strategy for increasing college success rates.

Transition from High School to College

Low rates of student success in college have been well documented. Less than 50 percent of new college students earn an associate's degree within three years or a bachelor's degree within six [Provasnik and Planty 2008; National Center for Education Statistics (NCES) 2011]. According to the National Center for Education Statistics (2011), 25 percent of full-time freshmen at

New Directions for Higher Education, no. 158, Summer 2012 © Wiley Periodicals, Inc.
Published online in Wiley Online Library (wileyonlinelibrary.com) • DOI:10.1002/he.20011

four-year institutions and 39 percent at two-year institutions do not return the following fall. The rates are even lower for part-time students.

To some extent, poor postsecondary outcomes are related to low levels of academic preparation (Roksa et al. 2009; Bailey, Jeong, and Cho 2010; NCES 2011). But even students who are ostensibly academically prepared struggle to persist in college. For example, a recent study of one cohort of first-time community college students in Virginia found that nearly 25 percent of students who enroll in a first-level college-credit English or math course do not pass (Roksa et al. 2009). In one cohort of new Virginia community college students, barely more than one-third of those who did *not* place into developmental coursework earned a credential within four years (personal communication with S. W. Cho, June 2011). That academically proficient students also have trouble persisting in college indicates that college readiness encompasses more than academic skill.

It is not a new notion that a successful college transition requires additional forms of knowledge. Researchers such as Attinasi (1989), Dickie and Farrell (1991), and Shields (2002) found that, among other things, new college students must learn to navigate a complex system of bureaucratic requirements, learn new study habits and time-management strategies, and engage in new kinds of social relationships. Students who do not have this knowledge are unlikely to be successful in college, even if they have the required academic skills.

Recently, authors and policymakers have refined this argument and tried to specify the types of nonacademic knowledge and skills necessary for successful secondary–postsecondary transitions. Conley (2005, 2007, 2010) presents a model of college readiness that includes academic content, academic behaviors, cognitive strategies such as analytic thinking, and "contextual skills and awareness" such as understanding college culture and processes. Byrd and MacDonald (2005) find that students who successfully make the transition to college have strong time-management skills and goal orientation, can advocate for themselves in order to get help, and understand college systems and procedures.

There is evidence that helping students learn the nonacademic facets of postsecondary education can lead to academic success. Most tellingly, studies of student success courses, which aim to help students acclimate to college, find that they positively influence student outcomes (Derby 2007; Cho et al. 2010; Zeidenberg, Jenkins, and Calcagno 2010): they improve academic outcomes without specifically focusing on academics, thus suggesting that college preparation must be viewed broadly.

Dual Enrollment's Social Dimension: A Theoretical Framework

Dual enrollment can be seen as a social intervention in which potential college students learn about the norms, interpersonal interactions, and behaviors expected for college success. By "trying on" the role of a college student, dual enrollees benefit from early exposure and practice, coming to feel comfortable in a college environment and ultimately becoming successful once they matriculate.

In sociological terms, roles are the "parts" that people play when they interact with others. They include the behaviors and attitudes that go along with any socially identifiable position, such as a student or a parent. We all understand how people enacting certain roles are to behave and that, if they do not adhere to these expectations, we are likely to view them negatively. Any time a person takes on a new role, she needs to learn how to enact it or learn the behaviors and attitudes a person who is playing her new "part" is expected to demonstrate.

The transition into a new role can be smoothed by various processes. One, *anticipatory socialization*, helps individuals learn about the broad set of behaviors, attitudes, and values of those who inhabit the role to which they aspire (Merton 1957; Ebaugh 1988). Anticipatory socialization happens in many ways, from daydreaming about the new role to watching others who already embody it, but it does not always provide the opportunity to practice a role. *Role rehearsal* does. A form of learning by doing, this second process occurs when someone has a chance to act temporarily as though he were already in a new role. Through internships, apprenticeships, or even activities like babysitting, individuals learn role-related expectations by trying to act accordingly and gauging others' reactions to their attempts to do so.

We can conceive of dual enrollment as an opportunity for anticipatory socialization and role rehearsal. Dual enrollees get ready for college success by learning—before they actually matriculate—*all* aspects of the college role. They acquire the technical demands of how to do college-level work. They also learn normative expectations—the habits, attitudes, and behaviors of successful college students—and discover strategies to enact these expectations successfully by seeing how other people react to their "college tries."

Dual enrollment might support postsecondary success because, after learning about and practicing the role, students do not need to spend their initial months in college acclimating to the college classroom. They already know what is expected of them and have experienced the difference between high school and college first hand. When viewed this way, dual enrollment becomes a strategy that broadly addresses the secondary–postsecondary transition. It also becomes appropriate for a wide range of students, because even those with strong academic skills need help learning normative college behaviors.

Substantiating the Framework: A Study

To evaluate the framework, I engaged in a semester-long study of dual enrollment students. Data collected included a series of semistructured interviews with twenty-six high school students enrolled in dual enrollment courses offered through two community colleges in New York City and in-depth observations of those dual enrollment courses. All participants took their college courses on a high school campus and were taught by high school instructors certified as college adjuncts.

Participants were first-time dual enrollees, which enabled me to examine their understanding of the role of college student prior to and after dual enrollment participation. Students were juniors and seniors and enrolled in one of five dual enrollment courses. The sample included fifteen males and eleven females. Four students were white, two were black, seven were Hispanic, twelve were Asian (primarily southeast Asian), and one was multiethnic. Only eight students spoke English at home.

I interviewed the students three times: at the beginning of the semester to gauge initial perceptions of what it means to be a college student, at the middle of the semester to document their dual enrollment experiences, and at the end of the semester in order to revisit their understanding of the role of college student. In total, this study draws on seventy-six student interviews and eighteen classroom observations.

Data were analyzed using a case-construction method in order to determine changes in role conceptions. I coded students' knowledge of the role into four categories: none or little, idealistic or highly generalized, realistic but vague, or strong and accurate. I examined each case to see if students moved up the continuum between their first and third interviews; I then looked across cases to understand how and why changes in role-related learning occurred. The following findings were associated with dual enrollment.

Students in Dual Enrollment Learn about the Role of College Student. As one would expect, students did not start the semester with well-defined notions of what it means to be a college student. Only one student in the sample was able to articulate strongly college student norms and expectations. By the end of the semester, though, most students—seventeen of the twenty-six—had increased their understanding of the role.

During Maria's first interview, she was barely able to describe a college student, and what she did know was very general and uncertain.

> [College students] could pick like what times they wanna go in and what times they wanna leave. They can go to class if they want, or not, and I guess, the teachers don't really mark them there. Or something. They have to do their homework and the projects or whatever. . . . They're more mature, I'm guessing.

When probed for more detail, she exclaimed, "I don't know, I've never been to college!"

By the end of the semester Maria was able to describe the role in much more detail. In her case report, her initial knowledge could be summarized

NEW DIRECTIONS FOR HIGHER EDUCATION • DOI:10.1002/he

in three short paragraphs; it took nearly a page to do so at semester's end. In her third interview, she also touched on a range of skills, behaviors, and attitudes required of college students, and—perhaps most important—was able to provide strategies for college success. She knew, for example, that college students are not coddled like high school students; therefore, they must seek out help.

In classroom observations, it was clear that some dual enrollment courses more than others closely mirrored the demands of classes on college campuses. Well-implemented dual enrollment courses reflected the content and pedagogical structures of high-quality, equivalent courses offered on the college campus. They therefore provided students with more authentic opportunities to practice the role of college student and were better at making the difference between high school and college visible to students. Students in these "authentic" courses were expected to complete work independently, engage in complex and analytic discussions, and take responsibility for their own learning by doing things such as following a syllabus. In authentic courses, students are required to engage in what are most likely new behaviors, and they experience a variety of new norms and expectations.

In contrast, students in "inauthentic" courses were generally given fewer opportunities to practice responsibility; for example, they were given notes instead of taking them on their own. Inauthentic courses also usually had fewer assignments and less interpersonal interaction around academic and intellectual topics. Not surprisingly, 80 percent of students in authentic courses increased their understanding of the role whereas only 45 percent of students in inauthentic courses did so.

Dual Enrollment Helps Students Practice College Expectations. Many students did not only learn about college expectations in their dual enrollment course; they actively practiced behaviors that helped them adhere to these expectations. Engaging in role rehearsal was strongly related to increased understanding of what it means to be a college student and how to be successful in postsecondary education.

Raul started the semester with an idealistic and not very useful understanding of what it means to be in college. At one point, he even noted that it is "better" to have classes back to back during the day, because "you probably stay in school two, three hours and then you go, leave. . . . And you actually get to go home, have your nap and relax. Wake up and do whatever it is you gotta do. Watch TV."

Through his college course, however, Raul discovered that successful college students take responsibility for their own learning. He began to review his notes on his own in order to keep up with the quick pace of the course. He took the initiative to get notes from his friend when he was absent. By the end of the semester, Raul was taking such responsibility for his coursework that he came to class even when his mother was in the hospital.

This practice translated into a new understanding of what it means to be a college student. In his third interview, Raul explained that in college, "you gotta do it [be academically successful] all on your own." He added that college students' success "all depends on how willing they are, or independent and committed they are to getting a good grade. . . . They gotta keep it in their head, 'I gotta study, gotta come to class, gotta do my work, gotta pay attention.'" This is quite a different image from the one he gave previously.

It is important to note that Raul did not learn about the expectations college professors have of their students because someone told him about them or because he observed others engage in them. Rather, he experienced them for himself: he was expected to act as a college student and came to understand the demands placed upon role incumbents.

Both role rehearsal and anticipatory socialization helped students learn about the college student role by exposing them to role-related expectations. This exposure came from the explicit and implicit demands made by their dual enrollment instructor, the feedback students received on their course performance from the instructor and their peers, and classroom norms developed by the instructor and peers. Students generalized these experiences to their broader image of "college student." It should be noted that, although authentic courses were more effective in transmitting this type of learning, students in all dual enrollment courses in this study increased their role-related learning, and no student ended the semester with a more poorly formed or more inaccurate role conception than the one held at the beginning.

Conclusions and Implications

As we focus on increasing college completion rates, it is important to remember that college readiness entails more than academic skill. Successful college students learn new ways of behaving, thinking, and interacting with others. Helping all students understand these expectations and learn how to live up to them is likely to increase the number who make it to college graduation. Dual enrollment is a strategy that can help provide students with such knowledge.

Given this broader understanding of college readiness and the role dual enrollment can play, policymakers and practitioners should consider a few things.

Authenticity Matters. Role-related learning is dependent upon students actually experiencing the college student role, and they cannot do this in courses that do not accurately reflect the expectations placed on college students. Practitioners often pay close attention to making sure that the academic component of dual enrollment courses mirrors those of on-campus college courses. But the findings presented here indicate that broader attention should be paid so that the normative, behavioral, and attitudinal expectations of dual enrollment courses reflect well-implemented on-campus courses as well.

Dual Enrollment—Thus College—Is Different from High School. Given the program's location on a high school campus, some students in the study did not grasp this difference; their role-related-learning was muted as a result. Finding ways to shift dual enrollees' experiences more dramatically, such as moving dual enrollment to the college campus or at least expecting students to spend significant time on a campus, is likely to increase the program's impact on college readiness.

Opportunity to Practice the Role. Role rehearsal is related to increased understanding of what it means to be a college student. Students not only need to hear about college expectations, but they also must be given ample opportunities to try them out. Practice gives participants the chance to understand truly what they need to do to be successful in their new role.

This last point has implications beyond dual enrollment. *All* potential college students need to understand the role that they are entering. As we turn our attention to college preparation in order to increase postsecondary completion, we must pay attention to the entire spectrum of college readiness. Dual enrollment and programs like it have an important role to play in helping students learn all facets of college readiness so that they may achieve their educational goals.

References

Attinasi, L. C. 1989. "Getting In: Mexican-Americans' Perceptions of University Attendance and the Implications for Freshman Year Persistence." *Journal of Higher Education* 60: 247–277.

Bailey, T., D. W. Jeong, and S. W. Cho. 2010. "Referral, Enrollment, and Completion in Developmental Education Sequences in Community Colleges." *Economics of Education Review* 29: 255–270.

Byrd, K. L., and G. MacDonald. 2005. "Defining College Readiness from the Inside Out: First-Generation College Student Perspectives." *Community College Review* 33: 22–37.

Cho, S. W., S. Jaggars, M. Karp, D. Jenkins, and N. Edgecombe. 2010. "Student Success Courses and Educational Outcomes in Virginia Community Colleges." New York: Community College Research Center, Teachers College, Columbia University.

Conley, D. 2005. *College Knowledge.* San Francisco: Jossey-Bass.

Conley, D. 2007. *Redefining College Readiness, Volume 3.* Eugene, OR: Educational Policy Improvement Center.

Conley, D. 2010. *College and Career Ready.* San Francisco: Jossey-Bass.

Derby, D. C. 2007. "Predicting Degree Completion: Examining the Interaction Between Orientation Course Participation and Ethnic Background." *Community College Journal of Research and Practice* 31(11): 883–894.

Dickie, L. O., and J. E. Farrell. 1991. "The Transition from High School to College: An Impedence Mismatch?" *The Physics Teacher* 29(7): 440–445.

Ebaugh, H. R. F. 1988. *Becoming an Ex: The Process of Role Exit.* Chicago: University of Chicago Press.

Hughes, K. L., M. M. Karp, B. J. Fermin, and T. R. Bailey. 2005. *Pathways to College Access and Success*. Washington, DC: Office of Vocational and Adult Education, U.S. Department of Education.

Kleiner, B., and L. Lewis. 2005. *Dual Enrollment of High School Students at Postsecondary Institutions, 2002–2003*. Washington, DC: National Center for Education Statistics, U.S. Department of Education.

Merton, R. K. 1957. *Social Theory and Social Structure*, rev. ed. London, United Kingdom: Free Press of Glencoe.

National Center for Education Statistics. 2011. *The Condition of Education 2011*. Washington, DC: U.S. Department of Education.

Provasnik, S., and M. Planty. 2008. *Community Colleges: Special Supplement to the Condition of Education 2008*. Washington, DC: U.S. Department of Education.

Roksa, J., D. Jenkins, S. S. Jaggars, M. Zeidenberg, and S. W. Cho. 2009. *Strategies for Promoting Gatekeeper Course Success Among Students Needing Remediation: Research Report for the Virginia Community College System*. New York: Community College Research Center.

Shields, N. 2002. "Anticipatory Socialization, Adjustment to University Life, and Perceived Stress: Generational and Sibling Effects." *Social Psychology of Education* 5: 365–392.

Waits, T., J. C. Setzer, and L. Lewis. 2005. *Dual Credit and Exam-Based Courses in U.S. High Schools, 2002–2003*. Washington, DC: National Center for Education Statistics, U.S. Department of Education.

Zeidenberg, M., D. Jenkins, and J. C. Calcagno. 2010. *Do Student Success Courses Actually Help Community College Students Succeed?* CCRC Brief no. 36. New York: Community College Research Center, Teachers College, Columbia University.

MELINDA MECHUR KARP is a senior research associate at the Community College Research Center, Teachers College, Columbia University.

4

This chapter explores how teaching in a dual enrollment program can foster new approaches to classroom pedagogy. Researchers from the Community College Research Center use qualitative data from California's Concurrent Courses Initiative to describe how program faculty implemented research-based pedagogical strategies in order to improve student persistence.

Teaching and Learning in the Dual Enrollment Classroom

Katherine L. Hughes, Linsey Edwards

Dual enrollment is viewed by many as part of a promising college preparation strategy for a broad range of students (Bailey and Karp 2003). But as participation in dual enrollment has expanded across the country, there has been increasing attention paid to the rigor and authenticity of dual enrollment courses, particularly for those courses held on high school campuses and taught by high school teachers [see "Standards" issued by the National Alliance of Concurrent Enrollment Partnerships (2011)]. Because dual enrollment courses are actual college courses that appear on a transcript the same way as other college courses, as opposed to college-level courses or curriculum such as Advanced Placement and International Baccalaureate programs, instructors are expected to maintain the standards, texts, and assessments of the sponsoring college or university.

The potential tension between broader access to dual enrollment courses and rigorous standards leads to interesting possibilities for innovative pedagogical practices. How can dual enrollment instructors uphold rigor *and* provide instruction and supports so that a broad range of students can be successful? Pedagogy in the dual enrollment classroom has been studied little, but answers to this question have implications for pedagogy in general at open-access postsecondary institutions such as community colleges, where some have argued that the quality of instruction has long been neglected as an area of study (Grubb 1999).

In this chapter, we draw on data from the Concurrent Courses Initiative, a multisite project that provided dual enrollment opportunities to disadvantaged California high school students within career-focused education pathways. As part of the project, a small number of dual enrollment instructors participated in an action research project in which they identified the

The authors thank the James Irvine Foundation for its support of this work.

NEW DIRECTIONS FOR HIGHER EDUCATION, no. 158, Summer 2012 © Wiley Periodicals, Inc.
Published online in Wiley Online Library (wileyonlinelibrary.com) • DOI:10.1002/he.20012

particular ways their students were struggling and then devised classroom strategies to address them. A number of insights and practices emerged that are relevant not only to dual enrollment instruction but to instruction at postsecondary institutions that provide broad access to students of varied academic abilities.

Background

In 2008, the James Irvine Foundation funded the Concurrent Courses Initiative (CCI), which provided support to eight secondary–postsecondary (mostly community college) partnerships in California as they developed, enhanced, and expanded dual enrollment programs that are rigorous, supportive, and career focused. The Community College Research Center at Teachers College, Columbia University oversaw and evaluated the initiative, which included a technical assistance component led by the Career Ladders Project, a California nonprofit that aims to improve postsecondary career pathway access and completion for underserved populations. The CCI specifically targeted low-income youth who are struggling academically or who come from populations historically underrepresented in higher education.

CCI sites varied considerably in terms of dual enrollment course location (on the college campus or at the high school) and type of instructor (high school teachers certified as adjuncts or college faculty), which was mostly due to local logistical considerations. This variation generated lessons about the challenges faced by high school and college instructors and the strategies they can employ to nurture student success. High school dual enrollment instructors often face challenges of how to define "college-level," how to find the appropriate level of rigor for their courses, and how to create a college environment. College faculty, on the other hand, who may be unfamiliar with teaching high school students, are faced with how best to engage them and what level of support to provide in order to ensure student success. As we observed CCI instructors grapple with these issues during the first year of the initiative, we found that many students were struggling academically and not persisting in their dual enrollment courses.

In response to these challenges, the technical assistance team devised a collaborative action research project for the sites. Instructors and others were invited to participate and work toward improving instructional practice for better student outcomes. The intent of the action research project was both to provide technical assistance to the sites and generate lessons on dual enrollment pedagogical strategies.

Action research methodology relies on the self-reflective practitioner as researcher, with the goal of improving practice (Kemmis and McTaggart 2005). This approach seemed particularly suited for the CCI because it provides a forum for instructors and other school staff to reflect critically on the needs of the students and change their practices in order to meet those needs. The collaborative nature of this approach provided the opportunity

NEW DIRECTIONS FOR HIGHER EDUCATION • DOI:10.1002/he

for sites to share challenges, successes, and lessons learned throughout the process.

The project was guided by a set of questions that helped participants identify a challenge they observed as it relates to struggling students. Each participant then chose a strategy to address this challenge, examined outcomes, and reflected on the impact of the intervention using an action research log. Each action research log was updated periodically and posted on an internal project Website that was accessible to all project participants. All participants were convened twice over the course of the school year (once in the fall, once in the spring) to discuss lessons and challenges and to brainstorm solutions with colleagues.

Challenges and Strategies

The challenges that emerged were of two general types: students' lack of academic skills and issues of students' affective adjustment to the college environment. These challenges are certainly familiar to those who work with or study community college populations; persistence and completion rates for these institutions are low for both academic and nonacademic reasons. For example, evidence shows that many students do poorly on placement exams, become mired in noncredit developmental coursework, and never progress to college courses (Bailey, Jeong, and Cho 2010). Some students are presumed to leave because of lack of involvement or integration in the college community (Tinto 1993), or because they do not feel sufficiently supported or validated (Rendón 1994; Barnett 2011). Action research participants addressed one or the other of these challenges or sometimes both.

Academic Challenges. Nearly all of the action research participants identified a lack of academic preparation as the primary barrier to student success in college coursework. For many students, a gap exists between their academic skills and the academic level in an authentic college course. This disconnect is partly a result of structural, cultural, and functional differences between high school and college institutions—where "the ways of knowing and intellectual norms" may be different (Conley 2007). These gaps make it challenging for high school students to grasp the material and be successful in college courses.

As many CCI action researchers indicated, the misalignment of skills is further exacerbated by students' lack of academic success skills, which makes it challenging to narrow this gap. These critical academic behaviors include out-of-class study, class participation, time management, stress management, and note-taking. Low basic skills combined with lack of academic behaviors negatively affect students' grasp of academic content as well as their confidence and persistence in their college course. Action research participants approached these challenges in a variety of ways: some focused their efforts on modifying their strategies within the classroom and others chose to add support structures beyond class time.

Affective Challenges. For comprehensive college preparation and subsequent adjustment, affective considerations—those relating to feelings and attitudes—can be just as important as academic ones. These considerations can be particularly important for students who come from families who have little experience with or understanding of higher education. Indeed, many of the students participating in the CCI had little emotional support from their families for their college aspirations, which made such support from college instructors and staff, as well as from fellow students, all the more essential.

Strategies for Student-Centered Learning. Many traditional college classroom practices operate via the model of active instructor and passive student (that is, teacher as lecturer and student as listener). Increasingly, however, practitioners and administrators are recognizing the potential of more active student learning for student success and pedagogy that takes into account students' history and needs—particularly for underrepresented groups (Kuh et al. 2006). Likewise, CCI action research participants sought to use these strategies to engage struggling students.

A multimedia course adjunct faculty member, for example, offered an extra credit project in which students were able to develop an individual project according to their interests. The instructor was impressed with the work these students produced when offered the chance to direct their own learning. Following this student-centered assignment, the instructor also observed increased motivation on a subsequent assignment. The instructor shared the vast improvement of one of his most challenging students:

> [The student] took initiative on the second film project, transposing his own scene from his favorite movie and organizing its shoot, finally editing it well—I'm not worried about his comprehension of curriculum currently. Listening to and validating [this student's] desire to shoot a particular scene yielded a terrific second production project.

In a similar vein, action research participants recognize the individual challenges students bring with them to the classroom and the need to be flexible and to customize their pedagogical strategies based on students' needs. As one instructor told us:

> I adapt the material using different examples . . . to tie it in to where they are right now in their lives. So that was the biggest adaptation, just trying to break down the concepts into language they understand . . . really the adaptation was about breaking down the terminology so they could get it. But the concepts were intact.

Multiple Means of Assessment. Although the literature on learning styles is vast and at times contradictory, researchers commonly agree that there are variations in student experience, traits, and preferences to a learning task that might necessitate the need to consider different ways students learn and process knowledge (Svinicki 2004). Multiple means of *assessing* that learning is an important consideration as well. The CCI multimedia instructor realized this after comparing outcomes from exams versus skills demonstrated on project-based assignments. In some cases, students who did poorly on exams excelled in their projects, thus leading him to believe that exams were not a sufficient means of assessing student mastery of content. He realized that "testing skills and production intuition are two separate things."

Instructional Scaffolding. Unlike pedagogical strategies, which may be implemented over the course of a semester, instructional scaffolds are more temporary supports used to help students achieve academic success. The intent is to decrease gradually the level of support provided as students demonstrate mastery. Action research participants used several different scaffolding strategies to promote achievement among their struggling student populations, including offering extra credit opportunities to increase grades, providing students with checklists to keep track of responsibilities, and presenting the information in smaller, more manageable pieces. Again, these strategies did not lower the expectations of the course but provided students with extra support to help them meet those expectations.

Academic Supports beyond Class Time. A crucial aspect of providing dual enrollment opportunities—particularly to struggling and underrepresented students—is the availability of a broad range of out-of-class supports that foster success. Indeed there is strong evidence to suggest a relationship between the provision of academic support services and persistence (Muraskin 1997; Brown Lerner and Brand 2006). However, such services can be a challenge to organize and are uncertain to attract student participation.

Among the action research participants, the most common means of providing out-of-class academic support was individualized tutoring. Tutoring was most successful when integrated into the program design or when used as part of a larger case management strategy. For example, as part of an introductory engineering course, college student tutors provided extra support to students during a mandatory supplemental instruction lab that immediately followed the class. At another site, staff integrated tutoring into a tailored case management plan for participating students and their families.

Validation of Students. Rendón's (1994) well-known work on validation emphasizes the importance of fostering "personal and social adjustment" (42) in students who are not from the traditional, more privileged college-going youth population. She defines validation as an "enabling, confirming, and supportive process" (44) that helps students feel worthy and capable of learning and developing. In the action research project, we saw significant understanding by the instructors that their students were in need of validation.

New Directions for Higher Education • DOI:10.1002/he

One instructor devised a way to address students' anxiety about being in college. At the beginning of the semester, she asked students to discuss openly what challenges they expected to face in the course:

> I then defined what internal and external roadblocks were and asked students to identify possible roadblocks that they had coming into the class or roadblocks that they may anticipate encountering during the semester. Once each student identified their respective roadblocks, we then collaboratively came up with lists of possible solutions and resources of whom or where they could go for help if they needed to . . . This strategy not only headed off possible problems, but it quickly showed the students that they were not alone in their struggles and that many other students had very similar challenges . . . They believed that we were going to be successful together.

Making Content Meaningful. A strategy relevant for addressing both academic and affective challenges is making education meaningful to students. As Duncan-Andrade (2009, 6) writes, "The most effective urban educators, in every discipline at every grade level, connect the academic rigor of content areas with their students' lives." Finding ways to make content meaningful and purposeful for students was a strategy many of the CCI action research project participants employed.

In several classrooms, instructors worked on ensuring that the course content was culturally relevant to the students in order to maintain engagement and promote achievement and persistence among the racially and ethnically diverse student population. In classroom activities, students were encouraged to use examples and analogies from their lives, which required a strong rapport between faculty and students, as well as trust among the students themselves. One instructor made a point to relate terminology and concepts such as assimilation and social privilege to the lives of her students. The courses that invoked this strategy had high student retention rates, with students reporting that they liked the opportunity to learn from their classmates as well as their teacher and that they appreciated the supportive and collaborative classroom environment. In implementing these strategies, however, the instructors did not sacrifice rigor. Using different approaches to help students understand the material does not necessitate lowering course standards.

Conclusion

Through the collaborative action research project, participating instructors were able to take a fresh look at the needs of their dual enrollment students, pilot some strategies to meet those needs, and share the results with one another. They were sometimes surprised at what they learned. One instructor said the project brought about an "epiphany" for her in that understanding the limitations and needs of her dual enrollment students also gave her new insights into the limitations and needs of her matriculated college students. A tenured professor who was teaching a cross-cultural psychology course, this instructor explained that, during the first several classes, students seemed to indicate they understood the material being covered, but she sensed that they really did not. As she shared with us:

> I decided to test their knowledge of vocabulary . . . I picked up the textbook and went through the first two chapters, and highlighted words that I would assume high school students would understand. I made a list . . . and when they came to class the next week, I asked them to take this little vocabulary test for me.

The results shocked her. Few students could define any of the words. For example, the first word was "comprehensive"; not one student gave the correct response.

Out of curiosity, she then gave the vocabulary test to students in her regular college courses, and they did similarly poorly. She realized she would have to change her approach so as not to assume students were familiar with the course vocabulary, and so she began to make a strong effort to define terms and concepts in multiple ways. She reflected on the experience:

> People are running around here [referring to her college] thinking that the students don't care, they're not motivated, it's because they're ESL students. You know what I say? They don't understand because they don't understand vocabulary. So now, because of that, I've incorporated vocabulary in all my classes. Students have to learn certain words, and I test them . . . We have dictionaries in the classes I teach. . . . a combination dictionary/thesaurus. . . . So that's just like an epiphany that I learned through this experience, thank goodness.

Her assumptions about the level of preparation of her matriculated college students were tested by her experience with high school students, and she developed a new strategy to help both student populations. The students attending her open-access community college are really not much different from the dual enrollment students, and, in teaching the latter, she gained a better understanding of the former. This lesson should have lasting benefits for all her students.

High school personnel had similar epiphanies. At one site, a qualified high school teacher taught a college introductory anatomy course at her high school, and, in the process, learned how underprepared her students were for the material. And as increasing numbers of students from that high school went to the college campus to take dual enrollment courses, the college faculty shared their perspectives on those students with their high school teaching counterparts. This dialogue led to additional cross-sector and schoolwide conversations on how to improve students' skills and facilitate a better transition from high school to college.

Ultimately, most students preparing to leave high school and attempt college need stronger academic skills and behaviors as well as emotional support and confidence in their abilities. Instructors, whether high school teachers or college faculty, are charged with transforming underprepared students into successful college students. The action research project demonstrates that professional development opportunities are instrumental in helping instructors understand the needs of their students and improve their pedagogy to meet those needs. Professional development as part of a dual enrollment program can have benefits beyond the program. Instructors must be encouraged to cross the high school–college divide since we require our students to do so.

References

Bailey, T., and M. M. Karp. 2003. *Promoting College Access and Success: A Review of Credit-Based Transition Programs.* Washington, DC: Office of Adult and Vocational Education, U.S. Department of Education.

Bailey, T., D. W. Jeong, and S. W. Cho. 2010. "Referral, Enrollment, and Completion in Developmental Education Sequences in Community Colleges." *Economics of Education Review* 29: 255–270.

Barnett, E. A. 2011. "Faculty Validation and Persistence Among Nontraditional Community College Students." *Enrollment Management Journal* 5(2): 97–117.

Brown Lerner, J., and B. Brand. 2006. *The College Ladder: Linking Secondary and Postsecondary Education for Success for All Students.* Washington, DC: American Youth Policy Forum.

Conley, D. T. 2007. *Redefining College Readiness, Volume 3.* Eugene, OR: Educational Policy Improvement Center.

Duncan-Andrade, J. 2009. "Note to Educators: Hope Required When Growing Roses in Concrete." *Harvard Educational Review* 79(2). Accessed November 1, 2011, http://www.unco.edu/cebs/diversity/pdfs/Duncan_Note%20to%20Educators_%20Hope%20Required%20When%20Growing%20Roses%20in%20Concrete.pdf

Grubb, W. N. 1999. *Honored But Invisible: An Inside Look at Teaching in Community Colleges.* New York: Routledge.

Kemmis, S., and R. McTaggart. 2005. "Participatory Action Research: Communicative Action and the Public Sphere." In *The Sage Handbook of Qualitative Research*, 3rd ed. Thousand Oaks, CA: Sage.

Kuh, G. D., J. Kinzie, T. Cruce, R. Shoup, and R. M. Gonyea. 2006. "Connecting the Dots: Multi-Faceted Analysis of the Relationships Between Student Engagement Results From the NSSE, and the Institutional Practices and Conditions that Foster Student Success." Lumina Foundation for Education Grant #2518. Bloomington, IN: Center for Postsecondary Research.

Muraskin, L. 1997. *"Best Practices" in Student Support Services: A Study of Five Exemplary Sites: Follow-Up Study of Student Support Services Program.* Washington, DC: U.S. Department of Education.

National Alliance of Concurrent Enrollment Programs. 2011. "Standards." Accessed December 1, 2011, from http://nacep.org/standards/.

Rendón, L. I. 1994. "Validating Culturally Diverse Students: Toward a New Model of Learning and Student Development." *Innovative Higher Education,* 19(1): 33–50.

Svinicki, M. D. 2004. *Learning and Motivation in the Postsecondary Classroom.* San Francisco: Jossey-Bass.

Tinto, V. 1993. *Leaving College: Rethinking the Causes and Cures of Student Attrition.* Chicago: University of Chicago Press.

Katherine L. Hughes is the assistant director for Work and Education Reform Research at the Community College Research Center, Teachers College, Columbia University.

Linsey Edwards is a graduate student in the Department of Sociology at Princeton University. Previously she was senior research assistant at the Community College Research Center, Teachers College, Columbia University.

5

How do dual enrollment programs benefit colleges and universities? Using quantitative and qualitative measures, the director of Kennesaw State University's Dual Enrollment Honors Program demonstrates the program's value to the university and highlights program concerns and challenges.

The Impact of Dual Enrollment on the Institution

Katherine N. Kinnick

As many dual enrollment programs enter a period of growing maturity, it is appropriate to ask about their impact on the institution. Does dual enrollment strengthen colleges and universities, or does it sap their increasingly limited resources? Does it make them better places to teach and learn? Does it increase their standing in their communities? What are the payoffs and trade-offs that colleges thinking about establishing or expanding dual enrollment programs should consider?

Proving the value of dual enrollment to the institution has become particularly important in recent years as the recession has squeezed state budgets for higher education. Programs that are not viewed as offering benefits to the institution become vulnerable in tough economic times. In addition, to operate effectively, all dual enrollment programs rely on the cooperation of a host of internal constituencies, from admissions to the registrar's office to financial aid and academic departments. Having these campus constituencies embrace the mission of dual enrollment helps build support for the program policies and procedures that are most conducive to the daily operation of dual enrollment programs. For these reasons, documenting the impact of dual enrollment programs on the institution should be incorporated into program assessment efforts.

Despite growing recognition of the value of dual enrollment on students' educational gains (see Chapter Two by Allen and Dadgar in this volume), we know little from the extant literature about the impact of dual enrollment on institutions of higher education. A study commissioned by the state of Rhode Island (Jobs for the Future 2006) addressed the impact of dual enrollment on the state's three public higher education institutions through interviews with key stakeholders, including college administrators,

NEW DIRECTIONS FOR HIGHER EDUCATION, no. 158, Summer 2012 © Wiley Periodicals, Inc.
Published online in Wiley Online Library (wileyonlinelibrary.com) • DOI:10.1002/he.20013

faculty, dual enrollment advisers, legislators, and business leaders. College administrators saw dual enrollment as a strategy to increase the diversity of their student bodies but expressed concern about their ability to ensure the quality of courses taught in high schools by high school faculty. College faculty shared these concerns, and they also viewed dual enrollment as having a negative impact on the institutions' revenues because students paid only nominal fees. State education officials and legislators held positive views of dual enrollment but expressed concerns about future funding. Business leaders were the most enthusiastic about dual enrollment, seeing it as a tool to move students through the educational pipeline into higher education and the workforce.

A survey of community college dual enrollment coordinators in Illinois (Barnett 2003) found correlations between program size and perceptions of benefits to the institution. Directors of programs with the largest enrollments were more likely to agree that dual enrollment benefits the institution by enhancing student recruitment, that dual enrollment is relatively easy to initiate, and that it is a practice associated with institutions considered aspirational peers by their home institution. The study did not establish a *causal* relationship between institutional attitudes toward dual enrollment and program size.

How we measure the impact of dual enrollment on the institution poses a number of questions. What are appropriate metrics for quantifying impact? How do we isolate important but more intangible outcomes for the institution, such as community goodwill, that are associated with dual enrollment programs? This chapter explores the benefits and drawbacks of dual enrollment from the institution's perspective using the case of Kennesaw State University (KSU). KSU's experience is offered not as a "best practice," but as an example of issues and challenges faced by many dual enrollment programs seeking to demonstrate their value to their own institutions.

Dual Enrollment at Kennesaw State University

Located north of Atlanta, Kennesaw State University is the third largest university in Georgia, enrolling 23,000 students and 200 dual enrollment students for the 2011–2012 year. Dual enrollment has been available at KSU and other state institutions since the 1970s. Georgia requires all dual enrollment courses to be taught by faculty from postsecondary institutions. Students must be high school juniors or seniors.

In 1994, KSU adopted an honors model for its program, now called the Dual Enrollment Honors Program (DEHP). Programs of this type are intended to provide strong students with an academically challenging alternative to the high school classroom (Rogers and Kimpston 1992). DEHP students must meet higher admissions standards than college freshmen: a 3.0 grade point average (GPA) in high school academic courses and a combined score of 1100 on Critical Reading and Math portions of the SAT. DEHP draws students from seven public school systems and more than thirty different high schools and homeschool programs each year. Most students come from large comprehensive high schools with a strong college preparatory emphasis; a smaller number come from high schools in rural counties with historically lower rates of college completion. A significant minority (currently 14 percent) are homeschooled students. Seventeen percent of students accepted for fall 2011 identified themselves as persons of color.

DEHP students take their courses on the KSU campus and are integrated with the general student population. Students may take any number of classes up to a maximum of seventeen credit hours per semester. During the 2010–2011 school year, 48 percent of DEHP students took a full-time load of twelve credits or more; most of these students did not attend any classes at their high schools. DEHP allows students the option to take college honors classes. Half of the students chose to take honors courses in 2010–2011, and they completed an average of 2.2 honors courses. To earn dual credit, students must choose courses from a state-approved list of courses that have been assigned a high school course code.

Funding. Two state funding programs offset the cost of dual enrollment in Georgia. The Accel program, originally tied to the state's Helping Outstanding Pupils Educationally (HOPE) Scholarship and funded by lottery revenues, was decoupled from HOPE for the 2011–2012 year and is now funded through a state appropriation. Accel is available to public, private, and homeschooled students and currently pays 100 percent of tuition, some mandatory student fees, and a textbook allowance of up to $150. Move on When Ready (MOWR) funding, initiated through legislation and implemented for the first time in 2010–2011, pays colleges from the state department of education's budget at the high school per-student full-time equivalent (FTE) rate. All public colleges in Georgia are required to participate in MOWR and to accept the FTE amount as payment in full for tuition and mandatory fees. MOWR prohibits students from taking any courses at the high school and requires that students take twelve credits of college coursework each semester. DEHP is also partially subsidized by KSU through the waiving of several mandatory fees, typically for services not used by DEHP students, such as a study abroad fund. Because of these fee waivers, Accel and Move on When Ready currently provide similar levels of support, meaning that most students will pay only the equivalent of textbook and lab fees.

Administrative Structure. DEHP at KSU is housed in an academic department, University Studies, which serves as an umbrella for a variety of academic enrichment programs ranging from learning support courses to the Undergraduate Honors Program. DEHP is coordinated by a staff of two: a faculty member, who receives a reduced teaching load to serve as program director, and a secretary. These individuals coordinate all aspects of DEHP, including recruitment, academic advising, orientation, initial processing of funding applications, communication with high school counselors, and coordination with academic departments and the offices of admissions, the registrar, and financial aid.

Measuring the Impact on the Institution

Like many states, Georgia has no systematic data collection program to gather information on dual enrollment from colleges and universities. KSU's efforts to measure program impact have been initiated internally, and findings are generally disseminated only at the campus level. Data are derived from campus databases and student and faculty surveys. They are reported in an annual assessment report and also used to complete program review documentation required periodically by the Southern Association of Colleges and Schools as part of the reaccreditation process. In addition, the data are sometimes requested by KSU's administration to aid in decision making related to program policies and funding.

KSU's experience reflects a number of methodological and pragmatic challenges for program administrators seeking to document their dual enrollment program's impact on the institution. Many dual enrollment programs are coordinated by individuals who do not have research backgrounds or statistical expertise. In addition, the daily demands of running the program may leave little time for assessment efforts. Data gathering may fall to offices of institutional research with limited staff and competing priorities.

KSU has found that the criteria emphasized by regional accrediting bodies in assessing academic programs provide a useful framework for assessing dual enrollment. Such program reviews are typically concerned with evidence of program quality, productivity, and viability. At KSU, evidence of positive impact is strongest in the areas of student recruitment, as well as retention, progression, and graduation. Although this is not surprising given the honors focus of KSU's program, previous research confirms that time to degree is shortened for dual enrollment students in a variety of program models (Blanco, Prescott, and Taylor 2007; Kleiman 2001; McCauley 2007). DEHP's impact on institutional viability from a financial standpoint is an area of strategic vulnerability shared by programs whose state funding formulas require institutions to absorb some program costs.

Program Quality. KSU's assessments help build a case that dual enrollment adds to the quality of the institution as a whole in three primary ways: through recruitment of high-achieving students, through enhancement of the classroom environment, and through positive impact on the image of the university as a school of choice. Data show that DEHP is an effective tool to attract students of high academic ability. Among students accepted for the fall 2010 semester, the average SAT score (Critical Reading and Math portions only) was 1205, compared with 1074 for other first-year students. Data from the past five years consistently show that a third of DEHP students reenter the university as first-year students. Exit surveys of 2010–2011 students indicate that 43 percent of reentering students say that their participation in DEHP led them to consider attending KSU when it had not been among their college choices before.

Surveys of honors faculty at the end of each term suggest that DEHP students enhance the learning environment in the college classroom by being good role models for other students. Survey data compiled since 2008 find that 86 percent of faculty indicate that DEHP students are more capable than typical first-year students, and 79 percent agree that they are more mature than typical first-year students. They describe DEHP students as hard working, attentive, prepared for class, and good natured. Ninety-three percent of faculty rate their level of satisfaction in teaching honors courses attended by DEHP students as high or extremely high. "It appears [DEHP] has some of the best and brightest students, which reflects well on both the participants and KSU," wrote one faculty member. Because of the characteristics of the students, faculty report being able to experiment with new assignments and activities, which further enrich the classroom environment.

DEHP also bolsters public perceptions of the quality of the university. Student exit surveys indicate high levels of satisfaction with the program. A majority of students (73 percent) indicate that the quality of instruction at KSU is better than the quality of instruction at their high school. Nearly 90 percent of participants say that they would recommend DEHP to younger high school students. There is evidence that they follow through: A quarter of prospective students who attend an "Honorview" information session say they heard about DEHP through a friend or relative. This word of mouth is especially meaningful when it comes from peers with reputations as top students. If top performers choose to attend KSU rather than the high school, and then in many cases reenter KSU, then KSU must be worthy to be considered a "destination" school by other students. Similarly, local publicity about DEHP students who are valedictorians, National Merit Scholarship finalists, or have other unique accomplishments confers credibility on the program and on KSU. Positive relationships developed with school personnel through DEHP build the image of KSU as actively engaged and committed to its community.

Program Productivity. How does dual enrollment contribute to the institution's retention, progression, and graduation goals? Research sponsored by the U.S. Department of Education (Adelman 2006) found that completion of twenty credit hours before the end of the first year of college is a strong predictor of timely college graduation. This research recommends expansion of dual enrollment programs so that all high school students can enter college having completed six college credits. DEHP participants well exceed this goal, completing an average of nineteen credit hours with an average GPA of 3.48 prior to high school graduation during the 2010–2011 academic year.

As noted previously, one-third of DEHP students reenter the university following high school graduation, providing a pipeline for KSU's Undergraduate Honors Program and graduate programs. Former DEHP students who graduated from KSU from 2008 through 2011 earned higher GPAs than other students who began college as freshmen in the same term. The average cumulative GPA for DEHP students at the time of college graduation was 3.4 versus 3.2 for other students. In addition, former DEHP students are significantly more likely to graduate in four years than other students. Of students who began as full-time freshmen from 2003 through 2006, 64 percent of students who had participated in DEHP graduated within four years versus 12 percent of other students. Former DEHP students are also more likely than the general student population to enroll in graduate programs and complete master's degrees at KSU (5 percent of former DEHP students versus 0.2 percent of students entering KSU in the same terms).

A limitation of this data common to many case studies of dual enrollment (Karp and Jeong 2008) is that it compares DEHP students with the general student population, rather than to students whose admissions scores indicate that they are of similar academic ability. Although controlling for academic ability would be ideal, this is not something DEHP staff has yet been able to accomplish given current campus resources and expertise.

Program Viability. Program viability is concerned with future demand for the program and financial sustainability given current and projected costs and revenues. Previous research has found that dual enrollment yields greater positive effects on the enrollment and revenues of two-year colleges than four-year colleges (Mokher and McLendon 2009). Move on When Ready funding for Georgia's two-year institutions is generally sufficient because of their lower tuition and fees. However, proving the value of dual enrollment from a financial standpoint is a more difficult issue for the state's four-year institutions. Although these institutions are mandated to offer dual enrollment since the passage of the MOWR bill in 2009, they take a financial loss on each MOWR student compared with other students. The state's per-student payment at the student's high school FTE rate ($1,439 per semester in 2010–2011) is only about half of current tuition and fees at most four-year institutions. At KSU in 2010–2011, the loss was $1,096 per MOWR student per semester. Because of this insufficient level of state support, as well as concerns that high school students may not have the maturity for full-time college work required by MOWR, some Georgia four-year colleges and universities have set extremely high admissions standards for MOWR students that have the effect of limiting enrollment. KSU also took a loss of $254 per student per semester in 2010–2011 on students choosing Accel funding. If KSU were to discontinue its current fee waivers for DEHP students, Accel students would be responsible for more than $500 in fees per semester, which could be expected to reduce enrollment.

KSU's losses are offset to some degree by the inclusion of DEHP students in KSU's enrollment headcount for state formula funding. For the

2010–2011 academic year, this funding was approximately $3,700 per student. In short, dual enrollment's impact on the university's bottom line is tenuous and, as in other states, current economic conditions and legislative priorities are not likely to increase state funding for dual enrollment.

The outlook for program viability is brighter from the standpoint of demand. Rapid enrollment growth (38 percent annually) over the last three years indicates strong interest in the program, which is likely to increase as the generous MOWR funding program becomes more widely known. There is demand from high schools that have cut course offerings due to state budget reductions, particularly in the area of foreign languages, or which have students who have exhausted the curriculum in a particular subject. There is also demand from homeschooling families looking for traditional, in-class instruction in particular subjects.

At the same time, public high schools have several disincentives to participate in dual enrollment, as they lose FTE funds for dual-enrolled students and lose enrollment from Advanced Placement (AP) courses, which lowers their ranking and prestige on a state "Education Scoreboard" that rewards schools for AP enrollment but not for dual enrollment (*Dual Enrollment, Advanced Placement, and International Baccalaureate in Georgia*, 2008). Anecdotal evidence suggests perceptions among some counselors that AP courses are considered more favorably in college admissions decisions than dual enrollment and that dual enrollment will remove the best students from the high school. Counselors may also dislike the paperwork and counseling time required for dual enrollment students. Nearly one-third (31 percent) of DEHP students noted in their exit survey that their high school counselors discouraged their participation in dual enrollment and in most cases encouraged them to take AP courses instead (see also Klopfenstein and Lively, Chapter Seven, in this volume).

From a community relations standpoint, dual enrollment responds to the concerns of families whose children have suffered from bullying or cliques in the high school, to the student who can continue to take Chinese after it has been cut by the high school, to the student who can pursue advanced math after she has "maxed out" the high school curriculum, to the elite athlete or performer who can arrange a flexible schedule to accommodate training, and to families who save thousands on college expenses. The ad hoc testimonies of these parents and students when they encounter KSU officials in the community cannot be underestimated. KSU's exit surveys indicate that the most highly rated factors in students' decisions to participate in dual enrollment were to "get out of the high school environment" (75 percent); "reduce the cost of a college education" (66 percent); and "reduce the amount of time spent in college or grad school" (66 percent).

Challenges to DEHP's viability relate to stresses caused by rapid enrollment growth campuswide and institutional buy-in. Parking and classroom space are at peak capacity. Department and college-level administrators may not see dual enrollment as relevant to their program goals; they may view DEHP students as taking seats from majors or students who need to graduate. Departments facing faculty shortages and under pressure to increase class sizes may resist providing faculty to teach small honors sections populated by DEHP and honors students. Commitment to dual enrollment from top administration is necessary in order to overcome these internal challenges. Although these issues are ongoing, DEHP assessment results have been helpful in gaining top administrative support.

Conclusion

The KSU example shows that relatively simple program assessments can provide evidence that dual enrollment programs have a positive impact on their host institutions. Proving positive impact may be particularly important for four-year institutions, which nationally are less likely to offer dual enrollment (Kleiner and Lewis 2005) and may see it as less aligned with their missions. The current environment faced by KSU and many dual enrollment programs reveals internal tensions caused by enrollment growth and resource scarcity as well as external tensions between higher education and public school systems that are exacerbated by state funding formulas for dual enrollment. Although proving impact of dual enrollment should be a priority in this environment, KSU's experience highlights the challenges of measuring impact without systematic support for data gathering and analysis.

The assessment measures employed by KSU are clearly only a starting point. The existing literature emphasizes the need for more sophisticated methodologies that can prove cause and effect relationships and overcome selection bias, a problem when more able students choose to participate in dual enrollment (Allen 2010). Such research requires funding and expertise beyond most dual enrollment program staff. Although the gold standard of random assignment of subjects to dual enrollment and nondual enrollment groups is rarely feasible, scholarship must control for academic and demographic characteristics of students, a limitation of KSU's data.

In Georgia, the lack of statewide data-gathering on dual enrollment means that each institution may develop different metrics for measuring program outcomes—if they are measured at all. Leading researchers in this area (Karp and Jeong 2008) have called for all states to collect comprehensive data, and for institutions to hire personnel with the ability to use it. Lacking state coordination, communication among institutions is needed in order to share best practices in program evaluation. The National Alliance of Concurrent Enrollment Partnerships (NACEP) is a resource for programs that use high school teachers to teach college classes; however, there is no similar organization for colleges with different dual enrollment models. The wide variety of program formats nationwide often makes it impossible to compare apples to apples and generalize findings. A final remaining issue relates to dissemination of information gained from assessment efforts.

What are the most effective ways for dual enrollment programs to get this information to key internal and external stakeholders and policymakers?

In states where colleges and universities are mandated to participate in dual enrollment, assessing the impact on the institution may seem like a moot point. Even in this circumstance, however, proving the value of dual enrollment to the institution is critical to internal support for dual enrollment, with implications for resource allocation, policy decisions, and advocacy for the program to other units on campus that can facilitate internal cooperation.

References

Adelman, C. 2006. *The Toolbox Revisited: Paths to Degree Completion from High School through College.* Washington, DC: U.S. Department of Education.

Allen, D. 2010. *Dual Enrollment: A Comprehensive Literature Review & Bibliography.* New York: Collaborative Programs Office of Academic Affairs, City University of New York. Accessed November 1, 2011, from http://www.cuny.edu/academics/k-to -12/databook/library/DE_LitReview_August2010.pdf.

Barnett, E. 2003. *The Diffusion of Innovations: Dual Credit Programs in Illinois Community College Systems.* Champaign: Office of Community College Research and Leadership, University of Illinois at Urbana-Champaign.

Blanco, C., B. Prescott, and N. Taylor. 2007. *The Promise of Dual Enrollment: Assessing Ohio's Early College Access Policy.* Cincinnati: KnowledgeWorks Foundation.

Dual Enrollment, Advanced Placement, and International Baccalaureate in Georgia: An Unbalanced Policy Environment That Short-Changes Student Success. 2008. Georgia Perimeter College. Accessed November 1, 2011, from http://www.gpc.edu/~je/the casefordualenrollment.pdf.

Jobs for the Future. 2006. *Dual Enrollment in Rhode Island: Opportunities for State Policy.* Report to the Statewide PK-16 Council. Boston: Jobs for the Future. Accessed November 1, 2011, from: http://www.ribghe.org/dualenrollment06.pdf.

Karp, M. M., and D. W. Jeong. 2008. *Conducting Research to Answer Your Questions about Dual Enrollment.* Washington, DC: U.S. Department of Education.

Kleiman, N. S. 2001. *Building a Highway to Higher Ed: How Collaborative Efforts Are Changing Education in America.* New York: Center for an Urban Future.

Kleiner, B., and L. Lewis. 2005. *Dual Enrollment of High School Students at Postsecondary Institutions: 2002–03* (NCES 2005–008). Washington, DC: National Center for Education Statistics, U.S. Department of Education.

McCauley, D. 2007. "The Impact of Advanced Placement and Dual Enrollment Programs on College Graduation." Applied Research Projects, Texas State University-San Marcos, Paper 206. Accessed November 1, 2011, from: http://ecommons.tx state.edu/arp/206

Mokher, C. G., and M. K. McLendon. 2009. "Uniting Secondary and Postsecondary Education: An Event History Analysis of State Adoption of Dual Enrollment Policies." *American Journal of Education* 115(2): 249–277.

Rogers, K. B., and R. D. Kimpston. 1992. "Acceleration: What We Do vs. What We Know." *Educational Leadership* 50(2): 58–61.

KATHERINE N. KINNICK is professor of communication and director of Pre-college Programs at Kennesaw State University.

6

A dual enrollment program administrator in New York City describes how program staff at seventeen two- and four-year colleges use a variety of data to set systemwide program priorities, to identify gaps in student participation, and to determine benchmarks for short- and long-term student outcomes.

Data-Informed Practices in an Urban Dual Enrollment Program

Jeanette Kim

Serving 20,000 students annually, College Now is the nation's largest urban dual enrollment program and represents the primary programmatic partnership between The City University of New York (CUNY) and the New York City Department of Education (NYCDOE). College Now's mission is to promote college awareness and strengthen the academic preparation of New York City public high school students by providing courses and activities aligned with first-year undergraduate study. With a belief that early exposure to college-level coursework would benefit the highest academic achievers *as well as* students from the academic midrange—students on track to graduate but not excelling in high school—the university expanded dual enrollment citywide in 1999 in an effort to give more students an experience that would prepare them for college success (Association of the Bar of the City of New York 1999).

Program Design and Administrative Practices

CUNY College Now is a familiar model for dual enrollment (Hoffman, Vargas, and Santos 2009; Barnett and Hughes 2010; Rutschow and Schneider 2011). This system-wide dual enrollment program provides students with multiple pathways to college readiness, offering opportunities to enroll in a range of courses and workshops and providing access to campus facilities. College Now uses precollege and postsecondary student-level data to inform program design; to set university-wide priorities, policies, and goals; and to work effectively with the diverse population of students and schools across the city. Research has found that students who participate in College Now are more successful in their postsecondary careers

New Directions for Higher Education, no. 158, Summer 2012 © Wiley Periodicals, Inc.
Published online in Wiley Online Library (wileyonlinelibrary.com) • DOI:10.1002/he.20014

(Karp et al. 2007; Michalowski 2007). The most recent study by Allen and Dadgar (using a quasi-experimental design described in Chapter Two in this volume) indicates that College Now alumni are retained at and persist in higher rates in CUNY than their NYCDOE peers who enrolled in CUNY but did not participate in College Now in high school.

A key factor in the success of CUNY's dual enrollment program lies in a keen understanding of the high school–college partnership. Over the past few years, heightened interest in the program's outcomes has led to an innovative data-sharing agreement between CUNY and the NYCDOE. For example, conversations about what it means for NYC students to graduate from high school ready for college have led to the development of comprehensive "Where Are They Now" reports produced by the NYCDOE. The reports provide high school principals with feedback on students' college preparation and aggregate outcomes for those who matriculate at CUNY. These reports have motivated school administrators to become more attentive to students' postsecondary outcomes. Furthermore, a recent change in the high school accountability metrics will measure the percentage of a high school's on-time graduates who successfully completed a college- or career-ready benchmark, such as earning a C or better in a dual enrollment course. Individual CUNY campuses, in turn, are interested in using College Now data to better understand their incoming student population and to develop targeted support structures for students who matriculate.

College Now is designed around a highly organized administrative, data, and reporting structure, and it functions as a single university-wide program that runs on seventeen CUNY two- and four-year undergraduate campuses. A central administration within CUNY's Office of Academic Affairs supports local program staff. A director at each campus manages the program, and most programs partner with fifteen to twenty-five high schools that are predominantly located in the geographic area surrounding the college. The director works with school leaders, counselors, high school teachers, and college faculty to administer day-to-day program activities. The Central Office staff provides curriculum and professional development for program faculty and staff, gives feedback to campus directors on program design, and conducts research on program implementation and effectiveness, as well as postsecondary student outcomes.

College Now offers a range of courses and activities, including college-credit courses, zero-credit developmental courses, precollege courses for high school credit, experiential-based summer programs, college advisory and awareness workshops, and access to campus facilities and student support services such as writing centers or tutoring centers. The majority of college course offerings typically fulfill undergraduate general education requirements, with the most popular being psychology, sociology, and English composition. Students enrolled in college-credit courses must meet minimum eligibility requirements via set scores on statewide English or math Regents exams, the PSAT or SAT, or, in some cases, a minimum high school grade point average. Requirements for some discipline-specific courses can be slightly higher at CUNY's senior (baccalaureate-granting) colleges. Programs implemented by community colleges often offer a broader range of courses, including developmental reading, writing, and math.

During the academic year, students participate in College Now through the partnership developed between their high school and host CUNY campus, for which there are two program models. The most common enrolls students from the same high school in College Now courses or activities that are scheduled either before or after school within the high school building. Programs incorporate some form of college connection by hosting an orientation or weekend activity that brings students to the college campus. This model makes College Now accessible to the greatest number of students in a single partner school. In the second model, participants travel to the college campus after school or on Saturday to take classes in a cohort of students from several different partner high schools. All College Now instructors are college faculty, adjunct instructors, or high school instructors appointed by college departments as adjunct instructors, an arrangement made possible by the New York State requirement that professionally licensed K–12 teachers hold a master's degree.

College Now also offers full-day, theme-based summer programs on the college campus, which are funded through a competitive application and approval process. These are often designed around a college-credit course and supplemented by an afternoon workshop that allows students to apply course content directly to an activity or project. Examples include the Bronx Civic Scholars Institute at Hostos Community College, which combines a college government class with practical experience interning in a community organization, and the Institute of Architectural Studies at the City College of New York, which combines a college introduction to architecture course with project-based, hands-on building and modeling experiences. Student outcomes are generally better for courses offered during the summer mainly because students focus on one area and not their entire high school course load at the same time. The experience is also more comprehensive than taking a single course.

Data analysts from CUNY Collaborative Programs (the umbrella organization for College Now) produce comprehensive College Now data reports to share with campus directors in the context of administrative and program management. These data, along with relevant research studies and topics, are presented and discussed during university-wide College Now coordinators meetings where practitioners address specific program management issues. At the end of each academic year, campus program leaders provide annual reports citing their successes and challenges around programwide benchmarks and goals and reflecting on their separate program outcomes and data. Each campus team has a certain degree of autonomy in its *individual* program design and activities while giving Central Office staff the ability to look across CUNY to set programwide goals and priorities.

Navigating Partnerships: Does Student Success Constitute Program Success?

In College Now, the school–college partnership is one that is nurtured and maintained over time. The goal is for each high school to be brought in as an active partner in program administration in order to help meet university-wide program priorities and goals. College Now partnerships afford high schools the opportunities for their students to participate in course sequences that would lead to college credit or build essential academic skills without an additional financial burden to the school.

The College Now program uses course and activity outcomes and College Now alumni postsecondary data in order to determine gains (or losses) toward programwide priorities and goals, to measure program effectiveness, and to ascertain the overall educational impact of the university-wide program. Although these measurements help drive program success for College Now, they alone cannot guarantee a successful program.

As an academic program, student outcomes are the primary indicator of program success. In recent years, approximately 75 percent of all College Now students were enrolled in college-credit courses. During the academic year, more than 80 percent of these enrollments resulted in a successful completion, which is determined by earning a grade of C or better. This figure jumps to more than 90 percent when looking at courses completed as part of the summer programs. By this measure, College Now is considered a success. However, given the complexity of the program—for example, the range of course disciplines, as well as the diverse profiles of more than 350 partner high schools, the seventeen colleges, and myriad instructor, student, and program model and partnership combinations—it is difficult to identify all the commonalities that can be used to measure success.

Enrolling a representative student population and implementing effective course sequences are additional factors in measuring program success. As a systemwide program, College Now continually looks for ways to shift resources responsibly to ensure support of activities that best address student success and equality issues, such as increasing the number of participants from low- to middle-performing high schools in traditionally underserved neighborhoods. Informed by school- and student-level data, Central Office staff discuss with campus directors specific program design strategies that will capitalize on effective high school partnerships. Campus-based program directors in turn meet with partner high school administrators and campus academic departments to determine program course offerings and recruitment strategies that will identify students who are not only interested and eligible for the program but who will best benefit from participation. This deep understanding of the high school landscape and strong connections with college offices have also contributed to College Now's success.

Enrolling a Representative Population

An analysis of College Now participation rates by borough during the academic year 2007–2008 showed a proportionally uneven number of students being served by College Now citywide. For example, 21.1 percent of all NYCDOE high school students attended a school in the borough of Manhattan, yet students from that borough represented only 12 percent of enrollments in College Now. Meanwhile, 24.2 percent of New York City students attended high school in the borough of Queens, but 33.4 percent of the total College Now enrollment was from this borough. These differences were more pronounced when enrollment data were grouped by gender and by race/ethnicity.

Central Office program administrators responded by reallocating resources systemwide so that serving a representative population across the city—with an emphasis on recruiting and retaining minority males—became top priority. This strategy has been vital to the viability of College Now programs working in the boroughs of the Bronx and Manhattan, and over the past five years, it has improved the participation of black and Hispanic males. In fact, the most recent data indicate a 27 percent increase in college-credit enrollments for black and Hispanic male students from high schools in these two boroughs (from 886 in 2006 to 1,129 in 2011) with a continuing upward trend in 2011–2012.

The latest descriptive analysis of CUNY outcomes for NYC public high school graduates with and without College Now experience shows positive differences across several categories, such as grade point average and credits earned in the first semester of college (see Table 6.1). Furthermore, bigger differences were seen in specific subgroups identified in program priorities, including males, black and Hispanic students, students scoring below 85 on the English Language Arts (ELA) Regents (85+ is commonly referred to as "mastery"), and students in associate-degree programs. If College Now enrolled only the highest academically achieving students in schools with large populations of "qualified" students, then the probability of student success (and to an extent overall program success) would also increase. However, this type of program design would not address the priorities of serving the midrange student or enrolling a representative population.

Challenges and Recommendations

Running and coordinating a program between the nation's two largest public urban education systems present many challenges and limitations—the most typical being adequate funding and resources. Given this context, the program uses student outcomes data, demographic data, and awareness of local and national educational policy in order to inform decisions on how best to distribute resources across the city. Current research on college access

Table 6.1. Differences in College Outcomes for NYC Public School Graduates with and without College Now (CN) Experience Who Entered CUNY as First-Time Freshmen in Fall 2008

| | N | | First-Semester GPA | | | First-Semester Credits Earned (FT Students) | | | Persistence to Third-Semester (FT Students) | | |
| | | | Average | | | Average | | | % of Full-Time Students | | |
	Non-CN	CN	Non-CN	CN		Non-CN	CN		Non-CN	CN	
Total Students	14,927	6,928	2.24	+0.32		7.99	+2.20		73.7	+9.50	
Gender											
Female	7,898	4,309	2.31	+0.31		8.12	+2.16		74.7	+8.90	
Male	7,029	2,619	2.16	+0.32		7.84	+2.19		72.5	+10.20	
Race/Ethnicity											
Am. Indian	47	20	2.03	+0.50		6.98	+2.52		66.7	+17.50	
Asian / Pac. Isl.	2,576	1,655	2.63	+0.12		9.85	+1.35		86.3	+3.40	
Black	4,086	1,839	2.00	+0.39		7.04	+2.17		67.3	+11.80	
Hispanic	5,859	1,984	2.12	+0.32		7.14	+2.28		70.0	+8.10	
White	2,359	1,430	2.49	+0.26		9.65	+1.66		79.6	+8.40	
ELA Regents Score											
Below 75	7,254	2,159	2.02	+0.23		5.77	+1.49		69.3	+7.10	
75 to 84	4,543	2,626	2.32	+0.24		9.75	+1.24		77.2	+7.90	
85 and Above	2,471	2,030	2.76	+0.15		11.54	+0.71		83.9	+4.50	
Degree Level											
Associate	9,996	3,291	2.01	+0.28		6.18	+1.78		67.9	+8.80	
Baccalaureate	4,852	3,622	2.68	+0.13		11.43	+0.65		84.7	+4.10	

and success, including postsecondary performance predictors (Adelman 2006), college-going perceptions and attitudes (Cox 2009), and advisory practices (Roderick 2006) are also used to shape program practice and implementation. Persuading high school administrators to look beyond high school graduation so as to understand the impact of College Now participation is just one of many conversations campus directors must facilitate. They work closely with their high schools to ensure that the "right" student—not just the one who is the most academically accomplished—is identified and recruited to participate in College Now. College Now data are also used by individual campus programs to help inform the status of the high school partnership and to identify appropriate courses and activities for students in each partner school.

Reaching Younger Students. In many College Now college-credit courses, students must meet CUNY's eligibility requirements, most of which are based on state or standardized exam scores. The timing of when a student takes an exam—the state ELA Regents exam might be administered at the end of the tenth or eleventh grade depending on the school and student—and how well students perform often dictate when and if they can enroll in a college-credit course. For example, a score of 65 is needed to meet minimum New York State graduation requirements, but a score of 75+ is needed to meet eligibility requirements for CUNY baccalaureate programs. In addition, analyses of NYCDOE districtwide high school enrollment patterns show significant attrition as students progress from tenth to eleventh to twelfth grade, a trend that is more pronounced in many of the city's struggling schools.

College Now precollege courses and activities were developed to provide alternative points of entry into College Now and to engage students who may not yet be ready to take college-credit courses but would benefit from a College Now experience. These activities were jointly developed by college faculty and high school teachers and focus on building and strengthening students' academic skills. College preparatory workshops, arts and music workshops, meetings with admissions and guidance counselors, and use of college libraries and facilities are other ways in which students are introduced to the college experience through this expanded dual enrollment program. In 2010–2011, the program generated 4,315 enrollments in precollege activities of twenty-one or more hours.

Small High Schools in NYC. Over the years, the growing movement to replace large comprehensive high schools with small, theme-based schools has challenged our approach to the traditional school–college partnership, especially in the area of recruitment. Although small schools may occupy the same building, each functions with its own administration, student body, and academic program. Simple logistics such as different bell schedules, classroom availability, and a smaller student body have complicated efforts to schedule a full cohort of students for a single class in a building that houses multiple schools. Carefully developed buildingwide relationships have enabled some College Now programs to leverage course offerings through structural changes at the schools, such as shifts in the school-day schedule or shared classroom space. For example, a section of Psychology 100 might be offered at the end of the school day by a single College Now program; students from all of the small schools in the educational complex would be recruited to fill a section composed of twenty-five students. Additional course sections can be added if each high school maintains its commitment to the College Now partnership.

Conclusion

Success in College Now is the result of a complex system of administrative structures that combine research and data analysis with attention to creative program design, rigorous program implementation, and robust high school–college partnerships. Careful attention to local and systemwide collaboration has made dual enrollment a significant driving force behind changing how the NYCDOE looks at schools' success in preparing students for postsecondary education. Starting in 2010–2011, College Now participation and outcomes will count toward DOE high school accountability metrics as one measure of college and career readiness.

College Now program practices and outcomes have also informed areas within the university on better understanding students' transition to college, particularly for the students with midrange academic abilities or those with remedial needs who comprise a large proportion of the student body at CUNY's community colleges (see Meade, Chapter Ten, in this volume). Conversations with faculty in college academic departments focused on pedagogical practices specific to high school students and effective curriculum implementation have been guided by an understanding of where College Now students struggle and how best to support them.

Going forward, we are exploring the best ways to bring multiple college programs to a set of schools in order to serve students with the program model that best suits their academic profile and ability to participate. For example, the majority of participants from high schools on Staten Island enroll in early morning dual enrollment courses offered at the high school through Kingsborough Community College. A smaller group of students participates in the afternoon on the campus of College of Staten Island (CSI). As a whole, CSI College Now participants show a higher academic profile, but more Kingsborough College Now participants matriculate at CSI. Understanding these patterns of participation and long-term outcomes is a new area of focus for the College Now program and promises to provide more carefully structured pathways for students of different ability.

References

Adelman, C. 2006. *The Toolbox Revisited: Paths to Degree Completion from High School through College.* Washington, DC: U.S. Department of Education.

Association of the Bar of the City of New York. 1999. "Report of the Commission on the Future of CUNY: Part I Remediation and Access: To Educate the 'Children of the Whole People.'" Accessed October 1, 2011, from http://www2.nycbar.org/Publications /reports/print_report.php?rid=47.

Barnett, E. A., and K. Hughes. 2010. *Community College and High School Partnerships.* New York: Community College Research Center, Teachers College, Columbia University.

Cox, R. 2009. *College Fear Factor.* Cambridge, MA: Harvard University Press.

Hoffman, N., J. Vargas, and J. Santos. 2009. "New Directions for Dual Enrollment: Creating Stronger Pathways from High School through College. Policies and Practices to Improve Student Preparation and Success." *New Directions for Community Colleges* no. 145.

Karp, M. M., J. C. Calcagno, K. L. Hughes, D. W. Jeong, and T. Bailey. 2007. *The Postsecondary Achievement of Participants in Dual Enrollment: An Analysis of Student Outcomes in Two States.* St. Paul: National Research Center for Career and Technical Education, University of Minnesota.

Michalowski, S. 2007. *Positive Effects Associated with College Now Participation for Students from New York City High Schools: Fall 2003 First-Time Freshman Cohort.* New York: CUNY Collaborative Programs, Office of Academic Affairs.

Roderick, M. 2006. *Closing the Aspirations-Attainment Gap: Implications for High School Reform.* New York: MDRC.

Rutschow, E. Z., and E. Schneider. 2011. *Unlocking the Gate: What We Know About Improving Developmental Education.* New York: MDRC.

JEANETTE KIM is associate director of College Now and director of the New York City Science and Engineering Fair at The City University of New York.

NEW DIRECTIONS FOR HIGHER EDUCATION • DOI:10.1002/he

7

What are the considerations when offering Advanced Placement or dual enrollment courses? In this chapter, researchers examine the history, structure, benefits, and challenges of each program in order to encourage schools and communities to think about the right fit when selecting a college-level transition program.

Dual Enrollment in the Broader Context of College-Level High School Programs

Kristin Klopfenstein, Kit Lively

In recent decades, as pressures have mounted to raise K–12 academic standards and move more students into and through college, high schools have provided a growing array of programs that offer college-level content. Frequent claims suggest that these programs raise academic standards, prepare students for college, and shorten the time to a baccalaureate degree, saving tuition costs and speeding entry into a career (Hoffman, Vargas, and Santos 2009; Klopfenstein and Thomas 2010).

This chapter compares the two most popular college-level programs, Advanced Placement (AP) and dual enrollment, and explains how choosing between the two is likely to be contingent on such varied factors as a school's geographic location and a student's academic profile and postsecondary aspirations. We also address how perceptions of AP's superiority have arisen from its popularity in top-ranked suburban high schools, perceptions that have influenced education policies and have led to the use of AP in schools where dual enrollment may be a better fit for students. Finally, we examine the efficacy of both programs in accelerating time to a baccalaureate degree.

The Designs and Uses of College-Level Programs

Parents, educators, and journalists who are familiar with Klopfenstein's research over the last decade on both dual enrollment and AP continue to ask which is better for students. They often expect to hear that AP is uniformly superior and so are surprised by the suggestion that the programs serve different populations with different goals and that each is important

New Directions for Higher Education, no. 158, Summer 2012 © Wiley Periodicals, Inc.
Published online in Wiley Online Library (wileyonlinelibrary.com) • DOI:10.1002/he.20015

in its own right. In fact, Klopfenstein has come to believe that they are better viewed as complements rather than as competitors.

In practice, the choice of dual enrollment versus AP is not available to the bulk of high school students in the United States. Typically, dual enrollment offerings are associated with proximity to a two- or four-year college, with the community college network tending to be geographically dispersed. For example, nearly 30 percent of community colleges serve low-density, rural areas (Provasnik and Planty 2008). In contrast, AP offerings are closely related to a school's size and the socioeconomic status (SES) of its families, with the broadest array of courses available, on average, in large, high-SES schools, which tend to be in suburban areas (Klopfenstein 2004). Because these suburban schools also are often close to community colleges that offer dual enrollment, the parents who ask whether their child should take one or the other typically reside in a large, suburban school district where access to both programs is taken for granted. In some schools, the choice between the two might even be procedural, as the student can take a single class that counts for either one or both. This leads to the perception among the teachers and policymakers who reside in suburban areas that dual enrollment and AP are competing programs.

Many curricular differences between AP and dual enrollment arise from their different designs, missions, and histories. Dual enrollment emerged in a decentralized way over the 1970s and 1980s to keep talented students challenged, help smooth the transition between high school and college, develop vocational readiness, and give students momentum toward a college degree (Burns and Lewis 2000; American Association of State Colleges and Universities 2002; Bailey and Karp 2003; Adelman 2006). Today, dual enrollment is as diverse as the state laws and individual agreements negotiated between colleges and high schools to govern the partnerships. Programs are located on college campuses or in high schools and are taught by college or high school faculty. Students earn college credit from the sponsoring college by fulfilling course requirements.

In contrast, AP was specifically created to allow advanced students who had exhausted their high school's course offerings an avenue to obtain credit for completing college-level work while still in high school. Originally conceived as enrichment for the most gifted students, precursors of AP arose in part from concerns about low standards in the general curriculum (Lacy 2010). AP still operates very deliberately today; it is run by a single organization, the College Board, which sets the curriculum and administers (through subcontractors) a standardized final exam. Classes are offered in high schools and taught by high school teachers, with students earning postsecondary credit or placing out of introductory courses only if their exam score meets the threshold established by a participant's college of matriculation. Although high schools are still more likely to reserve AP for only top students, enrollments in both AP and dual enrollment have diversified in response to reform pressures to raise academic standards in high schools and close achievement gaps (Hoffman 2003).

To understand the curricular differences between courses offered through AP and dual enrollment programs, it is helpful to understand how the AP curriculum is designed. For each subject area, the College Board surveys professors who teach first-year college courses and synthesizes the material into a single curriculum. Thus, AP represents an aggregate first-year course, filled with the content recommended by a diverse group of professors. In practice, however, very few college or university courses cover every chapter in the textbook; faculty typically teach the core concepts and then pick among the final chapters to emphasize areas of personal interest. AP, in contrast, needs to fulfill claims that students who pass AP exams can pass the final exam in a comparable class at *any* college or university. This approach puts pressure on AP teachers to cover copious amounts of material and has led to criticism that the curriculum is broad and shallow (National Research Council 2002). The College Board has responded by revamping its curriculum, starting with science, to focus more on depth of knowledge using best practices. Dual enrollment courses are less likely to suffer from the mile-wide-and-inch-deep charge to the extent that faculty are not constrained by a standardized exam and can select a subsample of topics on which to focus more deeply. The dual enrollment course *is* a college course.

Another difference between the programs is that AP teachers are not required to have any background, even an undergraduate degree, in the subject taught. For example, the bulk of AP teachers in economics, Klopfenstein's field, are history or political science majors who took just enough economics to meet the requirements of their university's core curriculum. When this happens, teachers might learn the material just slightly ahead of their students. (Fortunately, this issue is less pronounced in the most common subjects of AP English and AP calculus.) In contrast, most college faculty (and, by extension, high school faculty approved for dual enrollment instruction) have an advanced degree in the field they teach. However, this requirement does not guarantee that dual enrollment students will be exposed to high-quality pedagogy, for unlike certified AP teachers, college faculty members are rarely required to receive formal training in theories of teaching and learning.

Both dual enrollment and AP have unique advantages and disadvantages, depending on students' needs and postsecondary plans. Theoretically, any course offered through the participating college can be added to a curriculum, so dual enrollment tends to have more flexibility to serve students with a wide array of academic abilities—although this can vary with each local agreement (Burns and Lewis 2000). In contrast, AP typically offers only introductory survey courses, which focus on breadth of content over depth of knowledge.

Credit for passing grades in dual enrollment courses can often be readily transferred, particularly to in-state public colleges and universities, although there can be some logistical hoops and negotiation involved when applying credits to fulfill specific degree requirements. AP final exams may provide greater verifiability of academic quality than dual enrollment assignments and exams administered by local professors because AP vouches for content knowledge at each score point. Hence, out-of-state and private universities may be more willing to award credit for certain scores on AP exams, although there is no universally accepted "passing score." The College Board considers scores of 3 or higher, out of 5, to indicate that a student is "qualified" for college credit, but there is a move at many institutions to increase the required score to a 4 or 5.

We should also note that many high schools do not require students to take final AP exams, which are fee based, thus removing a measure of the course's quality along with the vehicle for students to earn college credit. But even taking an AP course without the corresponding national exam carries significant benefits, especially for students applying to selective colleges. High schools typically weight AP course grades more heavily than other course grades when calculating grade point average (GPA) and class rank, and AP classes on a transcript signal motivation and ability to college admissions officers (Breland et al. 2002; Hawkins and Clinedinst 2006).

The different relationships between high schools and postsecondary institutions can affect the ability of dual enrollment or AP programs to serve populations traditionally underrepresented in higher education. Dual enrollment is more directly collaborative because schools and colleges must have formal agreements delineating details such as which courses to include, where to hold them, qualifications of instructors, and requirements for earning credit. Partnerships also can improve communication and collaboration between the sectors around such important issues as curricular alignment and students' academic deficiencies—steps that can lead to reduced demand for postsecondary remediation (Edwards and Hughes 2011). With AP, relationships are more removed and generally facilitated by the College Board rather than by local institutional relationships. Similarly, although colleges have raised questions of academic quality for both programs, responsibility for responding has fallen to local programs for dual enrollment and the College Board for AP.

One potentially significant benefit for dual enrollment students is that the courses can be held at the participating college, engaging the high school students with peers who are actual college students in a framework that is college. Depending on the model, some of the main differences students may encounter are that classes can be large, they meet only a couple of times a week, attendance and homework are voluntary, and there are limited opportunities to display subject matter proficiency. In contrast, AP courses offered at the high school are typically quite small, enroll only other high school students, require daily attendance, and provide multiple opportunities for students to display their proficiency in class, including graded homework. The more genuine college experience of dual enrollment gives students an idea of what college is really like and of the importance of self-discipline, or as Karp notes in Chapter Three in this volume, allows students to practice being college students. But there is also less hand holding, which teenagers who are just learning to handle responsibility may need. Thus, whether a dual enrollment or AP course is best for any given student depends largely on the needs of the individual.

College-Level Programs and K–16 Reform

Perhaps the most frequent benefit claimed for college-level programs is that they prepare students for college. Accountability measures have been a major driver of such claims and the explosive growth of these programs over the last decade. For example, the No Child Left Behind (NCLB) legislation of 2001 notes that AP participants have higher SAT scores and high school and college GPAs, and thus NCLB seeks to "support state and local efforts to raise academic standards" by expanding the size and diversity of AP through federal subsidies to train more teachers, pay exam fees for low-income students, and build pre-AP programs in middle schools (Sec. 1702). These reforms presume that adopting the signature curricula of successful schools will be sufficient to reverse years of underachievement, but there is a risk of placing students in demanding courses without adequate preparation, as if high expectations alone can ensure success.

Although the AP curriculum does provide uniform standards, these standards are based on a college-level curriculum. In his original *Answers in the Toolbox* (1999), Adelman concluded that rigorous high school coursework is a strong predictor of college success, a recommendation that led many well-intentioned reformers to believe that all students in all schools, regardless of background and academic preparation, should be enrolled in the most challenging courses available. The claim that doing college-level work is good preparation for college may be true for students on the cusp of college readiness. But for students who are struggling with high school–level coursework, simply raising the stakes without a commensurate increase in support services is likely to end in frustration and failure. The focus instead should be on ramping up the K–10 curriculum so more students are prepared to do college-level work by eleventh grade (Dougherty and Mellor 2010). The Common Core State Standards, used properly, can be the first step toward a universally rigorous, developmentally appropriate curriculum for high school students. The standards, which lay out expected knowledge and skills across the K–12 grades, were developed through the coordination of the National Governors Association Center for Best Practices and the Council of Chief State School Officers and are being adopted by a growing number of states (Common Core State Standards Initiative 2011).

The common assertion that college-level programs help to shorten time to degree, thereby saving students money, is consistent with the original intent with which these programs were created (American Association of State Colleges and Universities 2002). Adelman (2006) highlights dual enrollment as helping to build students' momentum toward earning twenty credits by the end of the first college year, an important step on the road to degree completion, and the AP Website (College Board n.d.) asks, "Are you ready for a unique learning experience that will help you succeed in college?" However, there is little rigorous research investigating the claimed benefits of college-level programs and even less comparing outcomes for different programs.

Using Florida data, Speroni (2011) found that although dual enrollment participants were more likely to go to college than similar students who took AP, the AP students were more likely to enroll in four-year colleges immediately following high school. The dual enrollment benefits were found only when the courses were taught in community colleges and not at high schools. In a study of Texas high school graduates from 1997, Klopfenstein (2010) found that college students who had participated in dual enrollment graduated with a baccalaureate degree significantly faster than demographically and academically similar students with AP experience, and AP students graduated no faster than students who took no college-level courses in high school. Using a measure of simple degree completion rather than time to degree, Speroni found little difference between the college graduation rates of AP and dual enrollment students.

Klopfenstein's finding that dual enrollment students earn baccalaureate degrees significantly faster than other students is consistent with two possible interpretations: Either dual enrollment does a better job bringing along middle-achieving students, or students who participate in dual enrollment are stronger than AP students in terms of their unobservable characteristics, such as motivation. Although these two interpretations are not mutually exclusive, neither is consistent with the notion that dual enrollment is inferior to AP.

Given that there was little in the way of systematic supplemental supports provided for the subjects of the study—dual enrollment or AP participants who graduated from a Texas high school in 1997—it is hard to imagine the mechanism by which these programs would have accelerated time to degree other than the original purposes for which they were designed. Given the structural similarities between the dual enrollment and AP programs, however, we surmise that the bulk of the reason that dual enrollment students proceeded through college more rapidly was because of their determination to get through the degree program without delay in order to enter the workforce. This hypothesis should be tested using a mixed method research design and data that are both more recent and geographically diverse.

New Directions for Higher Education • DOI:10.1002/he

One finding of the study that could have some bearing on the results was that the demographic characteristics of Texas dual enrollment students were very different from those of their AP counterparts. Dual enrollment students were dramatically more likely to be from rural areas, to be eligible for free or reduced-price lunches in high school, and to apply for financial aid and work while in college. They tended to have lower grades in high school and college and lower SAT scores than AP participants. In the literature generally, rural residence and low income tend to be correlated with low test scores and low grades, so it is interesting to find that this pattern holds even for those students who pursue college-level work in high school. Speroni's (2011) result that AP students are more likely to matriculate directly at four-year colleges than are dual enrollment students is consistent with the demographic differences in program participants observed in Texas.

The Right "Fit" when Choosing a College-Level Program

Just as finding the right fit is important in college admissions, the same needs apply to identifying the most appropriate college-level program. Roderick et al. (2008, 71) define college fit as "a college that meets a student's educational and social needs and that will best support his or her intellectual and social development. Finding a good fit requires students to gain an understanding of what their needs and preferences are, and then to seek colleges that meet that description." For a student considering college-level options while in high school, this can mean weighing such factors as credit policies of the college she expects to attend, her comfort with attending class with college students, the strength of her academic skills, her willingness to work hard, and even what her friends are doing. Roderick et al.'s definition raises another important concept: Fit depends on students understanding their needs and finding a college that meets them. Again, college admissions offer useful parallels. Much has been written about the importance of social capital—guidance and support by families, communities, and schools—in selecting and gaining admission to the "right" college. To succeed in AP and dual enrollment, students need guidance to ensure they have adequate academic preparation before enrolling and ongoing support to ensure they understand how these programs operate as they navigate through whichever one they choose.

Dutkowsky et al. (2009) applied an expected benefit approach to the choice between AP and dual enrollment by weighing the likelihood a student will earn college credit against two potential cost savings if credit is awarded—the cost of taking a course in either program and tuition at the college the student attends after high school. The cost of an AP exam is cheaper than dual enrollment tuition. However, because the likelihood of earning credit can be higher for dual enrollment than AP, they find that dual enrollment makes better financial sense for students likely to earn average or below scores on AP exams or attend high-tuition colleges. They write that AP is a better fit for students likely to earn the highest AP scores, attend relatively inexpensive colleges, or secure large financial aid packages so that failing to earn AP credit would not create a cost burden. However, they warn that schools should not use these findings to justify limiting AP to only the most elite students; they recommend instead that schools with large college-going populations offer both programs to let students choose the option that serves their needs better. (It is important to note both that fee waivers are readily available for low-income AP test takers and that many dual enrollment programs are offered at no cost to students.)

In reality, the choice of dual enrollment versus AP is not available to the bulk of U.S. students. For students at small, rural, or low-SES schools, AP courses are scarce and, if offered, often fail to provide the well-prepared, highly motivated peer group that can make an AP class truly college like. Teachers at low-SES schools tend to be less well prepared, are often in their early years of teaching, and are most likely to be teaching out of field (Ingersoll 2002; Clotfelter, Ladd, and Vigdor 2006). Although AP courses are increasingly offered online, the combination of limited connectivity, intellectual immaturity, and a lack of structure, peers, and immediate supervision can make success difficult for many high school students, but particularly for those who will be first in their families to attend college.

Conclusion

College-level programs have evolved substantially in recent decades and are increasingly seen as necessary preparation for college among students across the ability distribution. The programs are also being used to increase standards in low-performing schools. High standards, however, are a necessary condition but an insufficient means for successful postsecondary preparation. These college-level programs can provide the target of high standards, but true readiness comes from the mechanisms through which students are supported in their efforts to reach college-level standards. The Early College High School model is one example of the use of dual enrollment as a target whereby curricular and pedagogical reform come through a multitude of supports used to address the unique challenges facing first-generation college students (see Edmunds, Chapter Nine, in this volume).

There is more than a nugget of truth to the claim that AP is the first national curriculum. Indeed, the use of college-level programs to drive high standards begs the need for a high-quality curriculum, such as the kind anticipated by the Common Core standards, which scaffold developmentally appropriate content over time. Until we have formally recognized national standards of high quality, dual enrollment and AP will partially fill that need. And because the two programs tend to serve different student populations in different settings and with different needs, it is unnecessary and unproductive to pit one against the other.

References

Adelman, C. 1999. *Answers in the Toolbox: Academic Intensity, Attendance Patterns, and Bachelor's Degree Attainment*. Washington, DC: U.S. Department of Education.

Adelman, C. 2006. *The Toolbox Revisited: Paths to Degree Completion from High School Through College*. Washington, DC: Office of Vocational and Adult Education, U.S. Department of Education.

American Association of State Colleges and Universities. 2002. "The Open Door . . . Assessing the Promise and Problems of Dual Enrollment." *AASCU State Policy Briefing* 1(1).

Bailey, T., and M. M. Karp. 2003. *Promoting College Access and Success: A Review of Credit-Based Transition Programs*. Washington, DC: U.S. Department of Education.

Breland, H., J. Maxey, R. Gernand, T. Cumming, and C. Trapani. 2002. *Trends in College Admission 2000: A Report of a National Survey of Undergraduate Admission Policies, Practices, and Procedures*. Accessed March 11, 2012, from http://www3.airweb.org/page.asp?page=347.

Burns, H., and B. Lewis. 2000. "Dual-Enrolled Students' Perceptions of the Effect of Classroom Environment on Educational Experience." *The Qualitative Report* 4(1/2).

Clotfelter, C. T., H. F. Ladd, and J. L. Vigdor. 2006. "Teacher-Student Matching and the Assessment of Teacher Effectiveness." *Journal of Human Resources* 41(4): 778–820.

College Board. n.d. "Choose AP." Accessed December 1, 2011, from http://www.collegeboard.com/student/testing/ap/about.html.

Common Core State Standards Initiative. 2011. Accessed January 4, 2012, from http://www.corestandards.org/.

Dougherty, C., and L. T. Mellor. 2010. "Preparing Students for Advanced Placement: It's a PreK-12 Issue." In *AP: A Critical Examination of the Advanced Placement Program*, edited by P. M. Sadler, G. Sonnert, R. H. Tai, and K. Klopfenstein. Cambridge, MA: Harvard Education Press.

Dutkowsky, D. H., J. M. Evensky, and G. S. Edmonds. 2009. "Should a High School Adopt Advanced Placement or a Concurrent Enrollment Program? An Expected Benefit Approach." *Education Finance and Policy* 4(3): 263–277.

Edwards, L., and K. Hughes. 2011. *Dual Enrollment Guide*. New York: Institute on Education and the Economy and Community College Research Center, Teachers College, Columbia University.

Hawkins, D., and M. Clinedinst. 2006. *State of College Admission 2006*. Alexandria, VA: National Association for College Admission Counseling.

Hoffman, N. 2003. "College Credit in High School: Increasing College Attainment Rates for Underrepresented Students." *Change* 35(4): 43–48.

Hoffman, N., J. Vargas, and J. Santos. 2009. "New Directions for Dual Enrollment: Creating Stronger Pathways from High School Through College." *New Directions for Community Colleges* no. 145: 43–58.

Ingersoll, R. M. 2002. *Out-of-Field Teaching, Educational Inequality, and the Organization of Schools: An Exploratory Analysis*. Seattle, WA: Center for the Study of Teaching and Policy University of Washington.

Klopfenstein, K. 2004. "The Advanced Placement Expansion of the 1990s: How Did Traditionally Underserved Students Fare?" *Education Policy Analysis Archives* 12.

Klopfenstein, K. 2010. "Does the Advanced Placement Program Save Taxpayers Money? The Effect of AP Participation on Time to College Graduation." In *AP: A Critical Examination of the Advanced Placement Program*, edited by P. M. Sadler, G. Sonnert, R. H. Tai, and K. Klopfenstein. Cambridge, MA: Harvard Education Press.

Klopfenstein, K., and K. M. Thomas. 2010. "Advanced Placement Participation: Evaluating the Policies of States and Colleges." In *AP: A Critical Examination of the Advanced Placement Program*, edited by P. M. Sadler, G. Sonnert, R. H. Tai, and K. Klopfenstein. Cambridge, MA: Harvard Education Press.

Lacy, T. 2010. "Access, Rigor, and Revenue in the History of the Advanced Placement Program." In *AP: A Critical Examination of the Advanced Placement Program*, edited by P. M. Sadler, G. Sonnert, R. H. Tai, and K. Klopfenstein. Cambridge, MA: Harvard Education Press.

National Research Council. 2002. *Learning and Understanding: Improving Advanced Study of Mathematics and Science in U.S. High Schools*. Washington, DC: National Academies Press.

No Child Left Behind Act of 2001, Pub. L. 107–110. (See Sec. 1701, ff)

Provasnik, S., and M. Planty. 2008. *Community Colleges: Special Supplement to the Condition of Education 2008*. Statistical Analysis Report. Washington, DC: National Center for Education Statistics, U.S. Department of Education. Accessed November 1, 2011, from http://nces.ed.gov/pubs2008/2008033.pdf.

Roderick, M., J. Nagaoka, V. Coca, and E. Moeller. 2008. *From High School to the Future: Potholes on the Road to College*. Chicago: Consortium on Chicago School Research, University of Chicago.

Speroni, C. 2011. *Determinants of Students' Success: The Role of Advanced Placement and Dual Enrollment Programs*. New York: National Center for Postsecondary Research, Columbia University.

KRISTIN KLOPFENSTEIN is executive director of the Education Innovation Institute at the University of Northern Colorado.

KIT LIVELY is associate director of the Education Innovation Institute at the University of Northern Colorado.

NEW DIRECTIONS FOR HIGHER EDUCATION • DOI:10.1002/he

Section II. Dual Enrollment Models That Strengthen School–College Partnerships

8

This chapter highlights policies and practices associated with two postsecondary preparation programs that use college placement exams and specially designed courses to create better alignment between secondary and postsecondary institutions.

Using College Placement Exams as Early Signals of College Readiness: An Examination of California's Early Assessment Program and New York's At Home in College Program

Andrea Venezia, Daniel Voloch

A promising strategy for promoting successful college transition and increasing college completion rates is to help students avoid developmental coursework by preparing them for placement exams before they enroll in college. A lack of content alignment between high school exit exams and college entrance exams is one of many troubling disconnects between K–12 and postsecondary institutions (Kirst and Bracco 2004). Low-income students, first-generation college-goers, and other traditionally underrepresented students are particularly vulnerable to the mixed signals sent by these conflicting exams and the lack of clear definitions around college readiness, as these students are the most dependent on high schools to prepare them for college success (Conley 2007). Given the research indicating negative correlations between the need for remediation in multiple areas and degree attainment, the lack of alignment between high school and college curricula, and students' lack of understanding of the importance of college placement exams (Venezia, Bracco, and Nodine 2010), it is vital that students are given an early signal as to their college readiness and are provided with opportunities to enhance their knowledge and skills before they graduate from high school.

California's Early Assessment Program

In 2004, the California State University (CSU) System, in collaboration with the State Board of Education (SBE) and the California Department of Education

NEW DIRECTIONS FOR HIGHER EDUCATION, no. 158, Summer 2012 © Wiley Periodicals, Inc.
Published online in Wiley Online Library (wileyonlinelibrary.com) • DOI:10.1002/he.20016

(CDE), started the Early Assessment Program (EAP). The main goal of the EAP is to increase the percentage of students who enter postsecondary education fully prepared to begin college-level study in English and mathematics. Students who score high enough on the EAP (or on the SAT or ACT) are exempt from taking postsecondary placement tests and can go directly into college-level courses. The initial impetus for the program was the high level of remediation in the CSU system. Even though all CSU students completed a college preparatory curriculum that is aligned with the CSU's eligibility standards, about half of the approximately 50,000 first-time students admitted to the CSU in 2007, for example, required remedial education in English, mathematics, or both.

The EAP is composed of three parts: the assessment, curricular opportunities for students that are aligned with CSU's expectations, and professional development for high school mathematics and English teachers. The EAP assessment items are part of the eleventh-grade California Standards Tests (CSTs, the state's K–12 standardized tests) in English and in Algebra II or Summative High School Mathematics. When taking these exams, students may choose to opt into the EAP and also complete a set of additional multiple-choice questions and a writing exercise. It is important to stress that the English EAP is available to all high school juniors, but the mathematics EAP is available only to juniors who have finished Algebra II or higher and are enrolled in a math class. Thus, fewer students take the mathematics EAP than the English EAP. In 2009, 169,473 students (77 percent of those who were eligible) took the mathematics EAP and 399,952 (82 percent of those eligible) took the English EAP (http://eap2009.ets.org/).

The EAP scores the test items as follows:

Exempt: Meets placement standards for entry-level college coursework and does not need to take a placement test.
Nonexempt: Not ready for college-level coursework and is encouraged to enroll in a senior-year activity to increase skills in preparation for postsecondary placement exams.
Incomplete: Not ready for college-level coursework because the essay or multiple-choice items were incomplete.
Conditionally Exempt (mathematics only): Currently ready. But, because many high school students do not complete a mathematics class in their senior year, skills and knowledge might decline. Students are encouraged to maintain their college-level proficiency in mathematics by participating in an approved senior-year experience. Students who successfully complete this experience are exempt from placement requirements. (Approved senior-year experiences are provided at http://www.calstate.edu/eap/documents/eapfaqfinal.pdf.)

During the first few years of the EAP, the main focus of the CSU's Chancellor's Office was on augmenting the eleventh-grade assessments and informing educators, students, and parents about this option. After the initial implementation of the EAP throughout the CSU system, the university turned a great deal of its focus to professional development opportunities for high school faculty. The CSU Expository Reading and Writing Task Force, comprised of members of the CSU, K–12 English teachers, and curriculum specialists, developed the twelfth-grade Expository Reading and Writing Course that high schools can adopt. The course is aligned with California's twelfth-grade content standards and is based primarily on nonfiction texts. The assignments emphasize the study of analytical, expository, and argumentative reading and writing. CSU campuses and county offices of education cosponsor professional development workshops for interested high school teachers ("Expository Reading and Writing Course" n.d.).

The CSU is developing a similar course in mathematics. Currently, workshops that provide professional development opportunities in the area of aligning high school math courses with postsecondary expectations are available for high school math teachers across the state ("Early Assessment Program: Frequently Asked Questions" n.d.). The CSU also offers a range of other preparatory materials and Websites, including online English and math lessons and tutorials ("Educators" n.d.).

The California Community College System. Remediation needs in the community college system are greater than in the CSU. Estimates of the percentage of community college students in California needing remediation range from 70 to 90 percent. However, placement in developmental courses is not mandated in California's community colleges so it is difficult to obtain accurate data (personal communication with Sonia Ortiz-Mercado, July 2011). In order to address the remediation rates for community college–bound students, in 2008, then Governor Schwarzenegger signed Senate Bill 946, legislation allowing California's community college system to implement EAP. This legislation provides authority to the California Community Colleges' Chancellor's Office to access data on students who take the EAP and—as of January 2009—for students demonstrating readiness for college-level coursework to be waived from their local community college's placement assessment (if the college chooses to participate in the EAP). Because no new funds were appropriated as part of SB 946, community college participation is voluntary ("What Is the Early Assessment Program" n.d.). As of fall 2011, fifty-five colleges used EAP data for placement purposes in English, mathematics, or both subjects.

In order to strengthen the use of the EAP at the community college level, the California Community Colleges' Chancellor's Office recently issued implementation grants to establish math refresher workshops and a college orientation course at Antelope Valley College; expand EAP, concurrent enrollment, and Summer Bridge opportunities at East Los Angeles College's South Gate Center; develop an Assessment Skills Building Program at Rio Honda College; and create a pilot project for an academic intervention for students who are conditionally ready at Shasta College. In addition, the Chancellor's Office recently funded Woodland Community College, Fresno

City College, and Santa Rosa Junior College to develop twelfth-grade and summer-bridge academic interventions to prepare students for college. Other funded pilots include the development of a twelfth-grade English course that is aligned with college-level coursework and provides students with the opportunity to earn college credit and an exemption from the college's placement tests if the students earn a passing grade.

EAP Data and Research

Although the CSU has not yet released large-scale data analyses regarding the impact of the EAP and implementation in the community colleges is still in its infancy, there are signs that the EAP is making a difference. A 2010 report by Howell, Kurlaender, and Grodsky used data from CSU Sacramento (CSUS) and the California Department of Education and found that participation in the EAP reduced the average student's probability of needing remediation at the CSU by 6.2 percentage points in English and 4.3 percentage points in mathematics. Given that approximately half of the almost 50,000 students who entered the CSU in 2007 needed remediation, these kinds of decreases could reduce the number of students needing remediation by about 3,000 in English and 2,000 in mathematics. In addition, the EAP appears to lead students to increase their academic preparation while still in high school; as important, it does not appear to discourage poorly prepared students from applying to CSU (Howell, Kurlaender, and Grodsky 2010).

Strengths of the EAP. The EAP is considered a major accomplishment in a state with virtually no centralized higher education leadership and rare examples of state-level collaboration across sectors of education. California has three distinct and separate postsecondary systems—the community college, the CSU, and the University of California—with no governing body that can make policy decisions across them, much less decisions that include K–12. In addition to the success of creating a common agreement and greater policy coherence, the EAP signifies to students, parents, and K–12 educators that academic readiness for postsecondary education is important and should be measured and remediated before students matriculate into college. It also created the space for researchers to collect and analyze data and for dialogue to focus on cross-sector issues.

One of the main goals of the architects of the EAP in the CSU Chancellor's Office was to find a key leverage point or anchor in the state's policy system, and they succeeded by connecting it to the California Standards Tests (CSTs). Although the CSTs will likely change soon (discussed next), the original conception was that, by aligning with the eleventh-grade assessments, the CSU would find a way to institutionalize and sustain the EAP over time. It also signals that students need to do more than pass the state's exit exam (geared toward grades eight through ten) in order to be academically ready for postsecondary education. Finally, it creates a space for professional

NEW DIRECTIONS FOR HIGHER EDUCATION • DOI:10.1002/he

development around issues that connect the state's public education systems (with the exception of the University of California). In fact, the Expository Reading and Writing Course is highly regarded across the state.

Weaknesses of the EAP. Although it made sense from a policy perspective to anchor the EAP in the eleventh grade CSTs, students need that information earlier in their educational lives—especially community college-bound students. Although the EAP might be able to help students who were conditionally ready and have taken the appropriate sequence of CSU-eligible courses, community college-bound students are often more than one year behind and consequently cannot catch up during their senior year. In addition, by the time high school students receive their CST scores in August before their senior year, it is often too late for them to change their course schedule or too late for their high school to offer new courses. Connecting the EAP in math to Algebra II prevents a large proportion of students from taking the exam; consequently, they cannot learn about their level of college readiness. The Chancellor's Office has funded EAP validation studies, but there are also questions about the validity of the EAP and whether it is reducing remediation, particularly from community college faculty who work in an environment in which each placement assessment must be validated in the local context of each community college's curricula (personal communication with Sonia Ortiz-Mercado, July 2011).

The EAP will change when a new assessment system aligned with the Common Core State Standards is implemented in 2014. If indicators about postsecondary readiness are integrated into the assessments that all students will take starting at an earlier age, schools will have a better sense of students' progression and receive earlier diagnostic information that can be aligned with coursework and professional development.

Finally, the EAP only addresses academic readiness and does not include noncognitive habits of minds and academic behaviors necessary for postsecondary success. For example, Conley (2007) indicates four dimensions of college readiness: key cognitive strategies, academic knowledge and skills, academic behaviors, and contextual skills and awareness. Students who take the EAP do not necessarily receive additional counseling, student supports, or exposure to other aspects of a college-going culture (see "College Tools for Schools" n.d. for examples of other aspects of a college-going culture). If their budget allows for it, the community colleges in California plan to start filling that gap by creating pre-EAP activities and reaching out to students as early as the ninth grade in order to provide them with information about college culture and expectations (personal communication with Sonia Ortiz-Mercado, July 6, 2011). As the next section discusses, The City University of New York's (CUNY) At Home in College builds on the EAP model by using college placement exams to provide early signals to high school seniors, while also offering academic support and structured advisement both before and after a student matriculates into college.

CUNY's At Home in College Program

In fall 2008, CUNY Collaborative Programs staff developed At Home in College (AHC), a college transition program intended to support students from New York City public high schools who were on track to graduate but had not met traditional benchmarks of college-readiness through statewide Regents exams or the SAT. The program emerged from work in College Now, CUNY's systemwide dual enrollment program. It was developed with an understanding that the majority of New York City public high school students who enroll in college enroll in CUNY and that the majority of these students require developmental coursework. For example, approximately 74 percent of students who entered CUNY's community colleges in 2010 needed remediation in at least one subject (Kolodner 2010).

Preparing Students for Academic Success. In order to prepare students for both the CUNY Placement Exam and introductory college-credit courses, CUNY faculty and staff in College Now developed a two-semester sequence of English courses. These courses, taught by high school teachers during the school day, provide a scaffolded approach to developing strategic academic literacy with a focus on nonfiction texts drawn from the fields of psychology and sociology. Throughout the course, students have the opportunity to complete assignments that mirror the CUNY Assessment Test in Writing, as well as longer, research-based assignments that reflect the writing expected in introductory college-credit classes.

In addition to the English course, two-thirds of participating schools are offering a yearlong math course. This course, which was developed by CUNY staff and faculty, aims to move students beyond a procedural understanding of prealgebraic and algebraic content and toward developing conceptual understanding, procedural fluency, strategic competence, adaptive reasoning, and a "productive disposition" toward math. Hinds (2009) provides an in-depth overview of the math curriculum used in AHC.

In developing courses that are explicitly aligned to college placement exams and that allow students to develop the targeted competencies necessary for college success, AHC helps students come to see how high school coursework lays the foundation for college success. At the end of each semester, students have the opportunity to take the CUNY Placement Exam. Traditionally, students take the tests once in late spring of their senior year; they are responsible for seeking information about the exams and materials that might help them prepare. Taking the exams for the first time in January provides AHC students with a clear signal of their college readiness vis-à-vis CUNY benchmarks, and teachers report that this signal helps encourage students to stay engaged throughout their last semester of high school in order to receive the structured support that will improve their college preparation. Pass rates on the various CUNY Placement Exams for AHC participants range from 10 to 20 points higher than the CUNY average depending on the exam and cohort year ($n = 2,100$), thus reducing the amount of developmental course-taking and increasing the likelihood of graduation for participating students who enroll in CUNY community colleges.

Providing students an opportunity to take the CUNY Placement Exams multiple times and discussing the importance of these exams (and the financial and academic consequences of failing them), AHC gives students a better understanding of why the exams are important. Knowing that these tests do not affect college admission decisions at CUNY, many students traditionally approach placement exams with little understanding of their importance, participating guidance counselors report. This attitude resonates with research that has found that, for most students, assessment and placement are viewed as an "isolated event that happens one day with minimal to no advance information" (Venezia et al. 2010, 2). Because of the tremendous cost of remediation to students and institutions, it is critical that students are made aware of college placement exams and the skills necessary to succeed on them as early as possible in their high school careers.

Professional Development. In order to develop a *comprehensive* college readiness program that addresses the different expectations of high school and college, it is crucial to bring high school and college instructors together to develop specific learning outcomes, assess student work, and create innovative curricula and lesson plans (Conley 2007). Through AHC, high school instructors meet monthly to discuss the curriculum, examine student work, and develop a stronger understanding of the expectations of college-level work. In addition, AHC has brought together high school and college instructors to discuss the expectations of "college-level writing," to implement a common assignment in both high school courses and college Expository Writing courses, and to discuss the feedback they provide to students. This has helped teachers develop an understanding of college-level work that moves beyond a superficial knowledge of standards to a more in-depth understanding of the quality of student work that meets these standards.

Helping Students Matriculate. In order to develop a structured approach to college application and matriculation, AHC developed a 30-week workshop. Each workshop is led by a high school guidance counselor who helps students complete college applications, file financial aid forms, and develop an understanding of the resources available on a college campus, as well as the bureaucratic structures that are characteristic of these institutions. During the summer between high school graduation and college matriculation, AHC students work with trained peer coaches (often alumni of the same high schools) who help students complete all of the necessary paperwork to matriculate successfully. This process helps strengthen what has been described as the "loose hand-off" between secondary and postsecondary institutions that results in significant numbers of low-income and first-generation students not enrolling in the college they planned to attend (Arnold et al. 2009). Seventy-three percent of students who participated in AHC in 2009 or 2010 and graduated from high school eventually enrolled in a postsecondary institution, which is considerably higher than the 58 percent overall college enrollment rate for the 2011 cohort of New York City public high school.

Using Existing Placement Exams to Signal College Readiness

Using existing college placement exams to provide signals of college readiness provides many benefits. Most important, taking these exams in advance of high school graduation may help to reduce the devastatingly high levels of remediation seen across higher education. There are, however, drawbacks to using these exams. For example, the reading and math exams used by CUNY currently provide little, if any, diagnostic information; students receive a score indicating if they passed or failed, but they receive no information that could help them improve their performance on future exams.

The ability of placement scores to provide clear signals about college readiness is complicated by the common belief that current exams are neither good indicators of the skills necessary for a student to be college ready nor precise instruments for placement. Citing an ACT report from 2006, Conley (2010, 11) notes that admission "and placement test scores are most useful at the extremes; students who do very well have the skills to handle college-level reading and mathematics. These exams are less useful for communicating to students the range of skills necessary to succeed in all entry-level courses or for determining the readiness of any individual student to do so." It is not enough simply to give a college placement exam as a signal, nor even to give workshops that solely prepare students for the exam. The experience of taking the exam must be followed with the opportunity to take courses that provide strategies for success on these high-stakes exams simultaneously with the opportunity to develop skills necessary for college success.

Conclusion: Supporting Students and Changing Systems

Although the potential exists for college transition programs like dual enrollment to serve as catalysts for changing systems, all too often the focus has been simply on providing traditional college credit courses to academically qualified high school students. According to McDonough (2004, 19), "college intervention programs aim to improve opportunities for individual students, rather than change the structure or functioning of schools, and thus are student-centered, rather than school-centered, programs. But this is an institutional problem, not an individual problem." There is a possibility, however, for these programs to assume the role of school-centered catalysts for structural change. Through programs like AHC and EAP, high school and postsecondary instructors articulate specific college readiness standards; develop learning outcomes and a common understanding of student work; develop benchmarks of college readiness; and implement clear college-readiness signals for students, families, and teachers (Hoffman 2007). Both EAP and AHC have worked on changing practices in the high school classroom and developing better alignment between secondary and postsecondary institutions so that students graduate better prepared for college success.

References

Arnold, K., S. Fleming, M. DeAnda, B. Castelman, and K. L. Wartman. 2009. "The Summer Flood: The Invisible Gap Among Low-Income Students." *Thought and Action* Fall: 23–34.

"College Tools for Schools." n.d. Accessed December 1, 2011, from http://college tools.berkeley.edu/.

Conley, D. 2007. *Redefining College Readiness, Volume 3*. Eugene, OR: Educational Policy Improvement Center.

Conley, D. 2010. "Replacing Remediation with Readiness." Paper presented at the National Center for Postsecondary Research Developmental Education Conference, New York, September.

"Early Assessment Program: Frequently Asked Questions." n.d. Accessed December 1, 2011, from http://www.calstate.edu/eap/documents/eapfaqfinal.pdf.

"Educators." n.d. Accessed December 1, 2011, from http://www.collegeeap.org/Educa tors.aspx.

"Expository Reading and Writing Course." n.d. Accessed December 1, 2011, from http://www.calstate.edu/eap/englishcourse/.

Hinds, S. 2009. "More Than Rules: College Transition Math Teaching for GED Graduates at the City University of New York." New York: City University of New York.

Hoffman, N. 2007. "Using Dual Enrollment to Build a 9-14 System." In *Minding the Gap*, edited by N. Hoffman, J. Vargas, A. Venezia, and M. S. Miller. Cambridge, MA: Harvard Education Press.

Howell, J., M. Kurlaender, and E. Grodsky. 2010. "Postsecondary Preparation and Remediation: Examining the Effect of the Early Assessment Program at California State University." *Association for Public Policy Analysis and Management* 29(4): 726–748.

Kirst, M. W., and K. R. Bracco. 2004. "Bridging the Great Divide." In *From High School to College*, edited by M. W. Kirst and A. Venezia. San Francisco: Jossey-Bass.

Kolodner, M. 2010. "Nearly Three-Quarters of CUNY Freshmen from City Schools Need Remedial Classes." *New York Daily News*, Dec. 15.

McDonough, P. M. 2004. *The School-to-College Transition: Challenges and Prospects*. Washington, DC: American Council on Education.

Venezia, A., K. Bracco, and T. Nodine. 2010. "One Shot Deal? Students' Perceptions of Assessment and Course Placement in California's Community Colleges." Paper presented at the National Center for Postsecondary Research Developmental Education Conference, New York, September.

"What Is the Early Assessment Program." n.d. Memo from the California Community Colleges Chancellor's Office, Sacramento.

Andrea Venezia is senior policy associate at WestEd in San Francisco.

Daniel Voloch is director of CUNY At Home in College. Previously he was director of the College Now dual enrollment program at Hostos Community College.

New Directions for Higher Education • DOI:10.1002/he

9

This chapter provides an overview of recent literature on college readiness and the emergence of the early college model. Using quantitative and qualitative data from an experimental study of early colleges in North Carolina, researchers describe the positive effects found on various indicators of college readiness.

Early Colleges: A New Model of Schooling Focusing on College Readiness

Julie A. Edmunds

Postsecondary educators have expressed concerns for many years about how prepared high school students are for college (American Diploma Project 2004). As a result, states and organizations have launched a variety of initiatives designed to increase high school students' readiness for college, including increased access to college-level courses. One of the most promising initiatives has been the early college high school model—an innovative high school–college blend that is purposefully designed to ensure that students are ready for college. Early colleges, as they are often called, expand the model of dual enrollment by incorporating dual enrollment courses into the whole structure of the school.

This chapter presents an overview of early colleges and their results, focusing particularly on how early colleges support the goal of college readiness. The first section briefly explores the concept of college readiness. The second section describes the early college high school model, and the final section highlights the impact of the model on different indicators of college readiness.

College Readiness

College readiness is a complex and multifaceted concept that includes students' knowledge and skills, behaviors, attitudes, and awareness of specific college processes (Conley 2007). A key component of college readiness is academic preparation: learning the content and academic skills that are necessary for success in college (American Diploma Project 2004). Studies have shown that the single most important predictor of college success is the

New Directions for Higher Education, no. 158, Summer 2012 © Wiley Periodicals, Inc.
Published online in Wiley Online Library (wileyonlinelibrary.com) • DOI:10.1002/he.20017

rigor of the courses that students take in high school (Adelman 2006). Taking the necessary courses needs to start in ninth grade. A study looking at high school transcripts in California found that only an estimated 6 percent of the students who did *not* complete Algebra I by the end of ninth grade completed the courses necessary for college by the end of senior year (Finkelstein and Fong 2008). Therefore, schools that want to increase students' college readiness must pay attention to the courses the students take starting in ninth grade to ensure course content is aligned to a high school curricular sequence that ends where postsecondary expectations begin.

In order for students to succeed in challenging courses, they need academic and social support (Swanson, Mehan, and Hubbard 1995), as well as emotional support (Savitz-Romer, Jager-Hyman, and Coles 2009). Academic behaviors such as study skills, time management, and the ability to self-monitor the quality of work are other core components of college readiness. Nonacademic behaviors, which include the ability of students to interact successfully with college professors and with their college peers, are also beneficial (Conley 2007).

A final key aspect of college readiness is awareness and knowledge of the specific procedural steps that students need to take to apply for and enroll in college (Tierney et al. 2009). This includes activities such as selecting schools of interest, taking the appropriate entrance exams, completing college applications, and completing financial aid forms—steps that have historically been challenging for low-income and minority students or students whose parents have never been to college (Roderick et al. 2008).

Ensuring that students are ready for college is thus more complicated than simply making sure that students take the right courses or take the SAT or ACT at the right time. Schools working on college readiness should focus specifically on developing college-ready academic behaviors and skills. Truly ensuring that a student is ready for postsecondary education requires a comprehensive effort.

The Early College Model

Early colleges are small schools that merge aspects of the high school and college experiences in order to create a new environment dedicated to increasing the number of students who graduate from high school and enroll and succeed in postsecondary education. The target population for these schools is students for whom the entrance into college has historically been more challenging, including students who are low income, the first in their family to go to college, or members of minority groups that are underrepresented in college.

The early college model as it is currently conceived owes its existence to seed money provided by the Bill and Melinda Gates Foundation, which started the Early College High School Initiative in 2002. Through the initiative, more than 230 early colleges in 28 states and the District of Columbia have been established (Jobs for the Future n.d.). Many more have been established outside the auspices of the initiative. The national initiative, which is supported by the nonprofit organization, Jobs for the Future, has established a set of core principles to guide the implementation of the early colleges. Early colleges that are part of this national initiative are expected to include the following core components (Jobs for the Future 2008):

A commitment to serving students underrepresented in higher education;
A partnership between school districts and institutions of higher education;
A coherent, integrated academic program that helps students get their high school diploma and 1-2 years of college credit;
Comprehensive academic and social support, coupled with college readiness activities; and
A commitment to advocating for policies that support early colleges.

Although many early colleges combine these components with a particular emphasis on early access to a college experience, schools across the country may vary in their structure and implementation of the model. For example, some of these schools across the United States begin in sixth or seventh grade whereas others start in ninth grade. It appears that the most successful of early colleges are using the notion of accelerating students' performance to reenvision the entire high school experience.

One such comprehensive model is being implemented in North Carolina, where more than seventy early colleges are in existence. The vast majority of North Carolina's early colleges are located on college campuses, and the college experience, including dual enrollment courses, is a critical component of the model. Beginning in the ninth grade, students begin taking college credit courses, starting with courses such as computer science, study skills, or physical education. Although many schools provide college classes in the ninth grade in which only high school students are enrolled, by the time students are in the tenth grade, they are often enrolled in college classes with other college students.

In North Carolina's model, the emphasis on getting students ready for college classes drives all of the other school components. As an early college teacher said, the school's mission is to "graduate students ready for college, career, and life. And you see it everywhere, and . . . so it's not even a motto anymore. It's ingrained in you, and that almost seems like your first response for what are you doing." Schools are thus expected to take a comprehensive approach to creating an environment that supports college readiness, including changing course-taking requirements, improving teaching and learning, building high-quality staff–student relationships, and providing academic and affective supports to students.

Key Research on Early Colleges

Early colleges are a fairly recent innovation; as a result, the research base is somewhat limited, but it is growing quite rapidly. In general, recent studies find positive outcomes for early-college students on a range of dimensions. This chapter focuses on two key studies: a national evaluation of early colleges and the first large-scale experimental study of the impact of the early college model. I spend more time on the second study, which has a rigorous design and establishes the most accurate estimate of the impact of the model.

National Evaluation. The largest study to date has been the national evaluation of the Early College High School Initiative. Funded by the Bill and Melinda Gates Foundation and conducted jointly by the American Institutes of Research and SRI International (2009), this ongoing evaluation primarily describes the implementation of the model and summarizes student outcomes associated with the model. According to the study, most early colleges were created as entirely new schools, were located on a college campus, and were partnered with two-year colleges. The early colleges were also enrolling the target populations, with two-thirds of the students representing racial or ethnic minorities and 59 percent from low-income households.

The national evaluation found that early college students did better overall than the other students in the district in which they were located. These impacts varied by the structure of the school, however, with higher impacts for those early college students who were in schools located on college campuses.

The national evaluation also found that early college graduates had accrued an average of 23 college credits by the end of their senior year in high school (approximately seven to eight college classes). After graduation, more than 40 percent of the students enrolled in a four-year university. The study team also conducted interviews with some students; they reported that early exposure to the college classes and the college readiness activities provided by the early colleges led them to feel more prepared for life at a postsecondary institution.

Although the national evaluation offers a broad examination of the program, the study team was unable to take into account students' incoming academic preparation or their motivation. For example, it is possible that early colleges were enrolling students who were already more academically prepared or who were more motivated and, therefore, would have done just as well in a traditional school setting. The next study addresses this concern.

Experimental Study of North Carolina's Early College Model

Working with colleagues at SERVE Center at the University of North Carolina, Greensboro, Abt Associates, and RTI International, I am leading a longitudinal,

NEW DIRECTIONS FOR HIGHER EDUCATION • DOI:10.1002/he

experimental study looking at the impact of North Carolina's early college model. Funded by the Institute of Education Sciences, this experimental study relies on the use of a lottery to select students for schools that have more applicants than seats. The study compares educational results for students who applied through the lottery system and were selected with those who applied but did not get in through the lottery. A lottery supports fairness and allows for a rigorous research design that suggests the two groups are comparable on characteristics such as incoming achievement and motivation.

The study investigates a variety of outcomes associated with college readiness, including high school achievement and course-taking, and behaviors associated with graduating from high school, such as attendance and continued enrollment in school. We also collect qualitative data on students' perspectives of the program. Schools enrolled in the study over time; by the end of the study, we will have results from more than 3,000 students in nineteen schools.

This chapter includes ninth- and tenth-grade results for a sample of a combined 715 students in the treatment and control groups who applied to attend six early colleges. Because we began following students in ninth grade, we do not yet have data on outcomes for large samples in the upper grades. In upcoming years, we will be able to report on outcomes such as graduation rates and enrollment in postsecondary institutions.

Rigorous Course-Taking. Results show that more treatment students are on track for college as measured by taking and succeeding in the core set of college preparatory courses. For ninth grade, we looked at English I and at least one mathematics course from the college preparatory track (that is, Algebra I, Algebra II, or geometry). In tenth grade, these core college preparatory courses include biology, civics, and economics, and at least two college preparatory mathematics courses. For each of these courses, we looked at the percentage of students who took the course *and also passed* the state-mandated test associated with the course, thus allowing us to capture both the proportion of students who had access to the course and how well those students did in the course.

As shown in Figure 9.1, a greater proportion of students in the early colleges (treatment) took core courses and passed the end-of-course test. These results were statistically significant at .10 or less only for the biology and the tenth-grade math course outcomes with this sample. We believe this is primarily due to the sample size, as analyses for our larger ninth-grade sample show that the ninth-grade math outcomes are also significant at p-values of 0.05 and lower. The results indicate that early college students are more likely to be taking the courses they need to be college ready (see also Edmunds, Bernstein et al. forthcoming).

Results reported elsewhere indicate that the program has a strong impact on outcomes related to students remaining in high school. For example, early college students were absent an average of 1.3 fewer days

NEW DIRECTIONS FOR HIGHER EDUCATION • DOI:10.1002/he

Figure 9.1. Impact on Core College Preparatory Courses

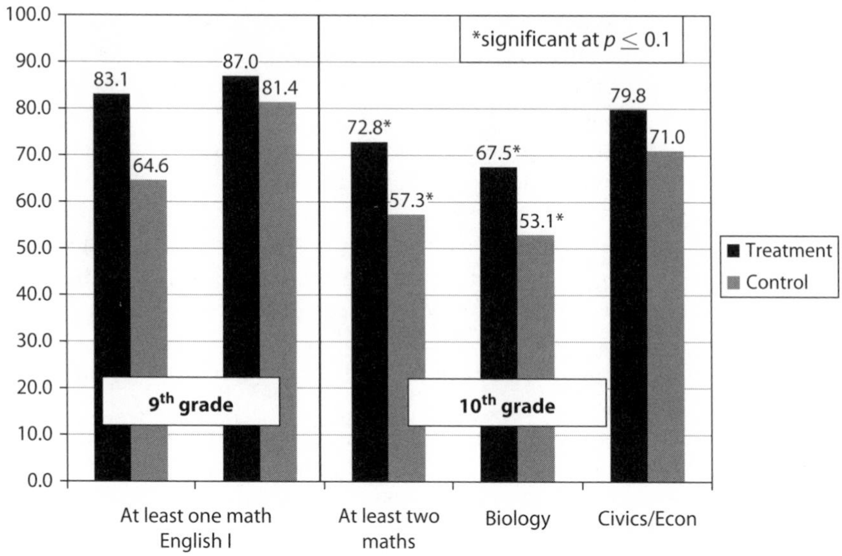

(p ≤ 0.001) and had been suspended half as frequently as control group students (6.5 percent suspension rate in the treatment compared with 13.1 percent in the control, $p \leq 0.001$) (Edmunds, Willse et al. 2011). Students were
($p \leq 0.001$) and had been suspended half as frequently as control group students (6.5 percent suspension rate in the treatment compared with 13.1 percent in the control, $p \leq 0.001$) (Edmunds, Willse et al. 2011). Students were also much more likely to remain enrolled in school, with 96 percent of treatment students still enrolled in a North Carolina school in tenth grade compared with 89 percent of control group students (Edmunds, Bernstein et al. 2011).

In addition to quantitative data, interviews with students and staff show how the early colleges have increased their students' college-going aspirations and their readiness for college. In addition, these interviews provide some insight into how the model's components are purposefully designed to assist students in becoming ready for college.

School–College Alignment. The explicit goal of early colleges is to ensure that every student is ready for college. This has resulted in increased expectations for the early college students and more rigorous high school classes, with all students expected to complete a college preparatory curriculum and all eligible courses taught at the honors level. Students saw the high school classes as being challenging in order to prepare them for the college classes they would be taking. A student at Lawson Early College (all school and college names are pseudonyms) said, "In high school classes, they go harder so when you take the college [classes], it'll go easier, so it'll be much easier for you."

Within the high school classrooms, early colleges tried to align their expectations and actions with college classrooms. The principal at Oak Early College highlighted how the school purposefully set up the teaching and learning in high school classrooms to mirror what happens in the college classroom and better prepare students for what they would encounter in college classes:

> As far as teaching and learning, it's about making sure that we mirror a lot of things that the college do. . . . Every single teacher here has a syllabus; whereas before, teachers just kind of had their pacing guide and their objectives and the students never saw it. But now, we have a syllabus. Students know exactly what they're going to encounter, so students are getting used to seeing what they're going to encounter on the community college side . . . our teachers have access to the syllabus [in the college], especially in the English and math areas, so our teachers know exactly what they're going to encounter.

College Behaviors and Skills. Students also commented that being on a college campus and taking college courses taught them some of the behaviors that were needed in college. A student at Hancock Early College said, "When we go out, you don't want to act like you're in high school. . . . Here [in the high school rooms] I'm a high school student. On campus, I'm a college student and they treat me as such." Students also believed that interacting with older students could provide them with lifelong skills that would allow them to do well in college and careers.

In addition to helping students learn to interact effectively with adults, the early colleges required students to take courses that focused on college-going skills such as study skills and time management. The college liaison at Fairdale Early College taught a college-credit course designed to prepare students for success in the community college. She described some of what she included in this course as follows: "I don't only talk about the study skills that are necessary but also the mind-set and the responsibility that they're going to have to take on their shoulders if they're going to succeed. No one's going to tell them when to get up. No one's going to tell them to go to class. No one's going to tell them to go to the Registrar's office and get their paperwork."

College Logistics. Early colleges also helped students with some of the logistical hurdles of attending college, not the least of which was free college courses for students, an aspect that was highly valued by many students. One student commented, "My family's on an extremely low income compared to most families, and if I hadn't come here, the opportunities for higher education would have been limited. So this school provided me opportunities that wouldn't have been available to my economic status otherwise."

The qualitative data described in this chapter highlight how a clear focus on preparing all students for college requires a rethinking of the basics of the high school experience. This has resulted in a different experience for early college students compared to those in traditional high schools, as shown by survey data we collected on the school experiences of both early college and control students: Early college students reported significantly more positive high school experiences on all of the dimensions we examined, including significantly higher academic expectations on behalf of the teachers, better relationships with their teachers, more rigorous and relevant instruction, and more varied and frequent support activities (Edmunds, Willse et al. 2011).

Conclusion

Early colleges represent an innovative approach to educating adolescents that is purposefully designed to support college readiness while eliminating the boundaries that currently exist between high school and postsecondary education. Because of the partnership between the high school and the college, early college students are simultaneously high school and college students. In one sense, early colleges provide an immediate assessment of whether students are college ready. For example, because the dual enrollment courses and the college experience allow both students and faculty to assess students' readiness for college, schools can, if necessary, revise the design and services to help students be more successful in college. This approach seems to be working well, as early colleges have been having a substantial positive impact on a variety of outcomes associated with college readiness. A student at Grayson Early College highlighted how being in the early college was different from solely taking dual enrollment in high school: "The thing with the high school is . . . you're in high school and you're taking some college classes, too. Here [in the early college] you are in college. This is like the end of the beginning . . . so then it just opens up a new pathway for us to keep going."

References

Adelman, C. 2006. *The Toolbox Revisited: Paths to Degree Completion from High School through College.* Washington, DC: U.S. Department of Education.

American Diploma Project. 2004. *Ready or Not? Creating a High School Diploma That Counts.* Washington, DC: Achieve.

American Institutes of Research and SRI International. 2009. *Six Years and Counting: The ECHSI Matures.* Fifth Annual Early College High School Initiative Evaluation Synthesis Report. Washington, DC: American Institutes of Research. (ED 514 090)

Conley, D. 2007. *Redefining College Readiness, Volume 3.* Eugene, OR: Educational Policy Improvement Center.

Edmunds, J. A., L. Bernstein, F. Unlu, E. Glennie, N. Arshavsky, and A. Smith. April, 2011. "Keeping Students in School: Impact of a High School Reform Model on Students'

Enrollment and Progression in School." Paper presented at the national meeting of the American Educational Research Association, New Orleans.

Edmunds, J. A., L. Bernstein, F. Unlu, E. Glennie, J. Willse, A. Smith, and N. Arshavsky. Forthcoming. "Expanding the Start of the College Pipeline: Ninth Grade Findings from an Experimental Study of the Impact of the Early College High School Model." *Journal of Research on Educational Effectiveness*.

Edmunds, J. A., J. Willse, N. Arshavsky, and A. Dallas. 2011. "Mandated Engagement: The Impact of Early College High Schools." Working paper.

Finkelstein, N. D., and Fong, A. B. 2008. *Course-taking Patterns and Preparation for Post-secondary Education in California's Public University Systems Among Minority Youth*. Issues & Answers Report, REL 2008–No. 035. Washington, DC: Institute of Education Sciences, National Center for Education Evaluation and Regional Assistance, Regional Educational Laboratory West, U.S. Department of Education.

Jobs for the Future. 2008. "Early College High School Initiative Core Principles." Accessed March 11, 2012, from http://www.jff.org/sites/default/files/ECHSI_Core_principles.pdf.

Jobs for the Future. n.d. "Welcome to Early College High School." Accessed December 1, 2011, from http://www.earlycolleges.org.

Roderick, M., J. Nagaoka, V. Coca, and E. Moeller. 2008. *From High School to the Future: Potholes on the Road to College*. Chicago: Consortium on Chicago School Research.

Savitz-Romer, M., J. Jager-Hyman, and A. Coles. 2009. *Removing Roadblocks to Rigor: Linking Academic and Social Supports to Ensure College Readiness and Success*. Washington, DC: Pathways to College Network, Institute for Higher Education Policy.

Swanson, M. C., H. Mehan, and L. Hubbard. 1995. "The AVID Classroom: Academic and Social Support for Low-Achieving Students." In *Creating New Educational Communities*. Ninety-fourth Yearbook of the National Society for the Study of Education. Part I, edited by J. Oakes and K. H. Quartz. Chicago: University of Chicago Press.

Tierney, W. G., T. Bailey, J. Constantine, N. Finkelstein, and N. F. Hurd. 2009. *Helping Students Navigate the Path to College: What High Schools Can Do*. A Practice Guide (NCEE #2009–4066). Washington, DC: U.S. Department of Education.

Julie A. Edmunds *is project director of High School Reform at SERVE Center, University of North Carolina at Greensboro.*

10

In this chapter, the former director of the New Community College Initiative at The City University of New York explains how dual enrollment programs influenced the development of an admissions process, first-year curriculum, and advisement structures at the new institution.

Dual Enrollment Lessons and the Development of The New Community College at CUNY

Tracy Meade

In March 2008, The City University of New York (CUNY) Chancellor Matthew Goldstein formally launched an initiative to create the university's seventh community college. The development of the concept for this new college is informed in part by the knowledge and practices acquired through working with high school and GED students. Specifically, this chapter describes how important elements of the concept for The New Community College at CUNY emerged from lessons learned through nearly ten years of developing a systemwide approach to dual enrollment in the university's College Now program. Through steadfast efforts to understand the range of student needs throughout the college transition process and the first year of college, the experience and expertise of College Now administrators, faculty, and staff contributed in substantial ways to the development of the concept for the new college.

The School–College Divide

Only 21 percent of New York City public school students entering ninth grade in 2007 demonstrated college proficiency four years later, and only 50 percent of these students enrolled in college (Santos 2011). Equally troubling, only 12 percent of full-time, first-time freshmen who enrolled in CUNY associate-degree programs in 2007 graduated within three years, with about one-third of the entering cohort still enrolled at that time. Enrollment, achievement, and degree attainment rates are particularly distressing for minority students and students from low-income households.

New Directions for Higher Education, no. 158, Summer 2012 © Wiley Periodicals, Inc.
Published online in Wiley Online Library (wileyonlinelibrary.com) • DOI:10.1002/he.20018

A confluence of factors—inadequate academic preparation, limited personal and financial support, and disconnected administrative processes—contribute to underperformance in college. For example, high school definitions of success are rarely aligned with college expectations. As Conley (2007, 10) explains, students "from low-income families are particularly vulnerable to a system that does not send clear signals to students on how ready they are for college." So although students exit high school assuming themselves college ready, at CUNY (and across the United States), a high percentage of incoming freshmen will not meet eligibility requirements in at least one of three areas: reading, writing, or mathematics. Thus the burden of a high school model that has not yet adequately addressed college preparation for *all* students falls on high school graduates who enroll in associate-degree programs and quickly learn that they must spend time in costly remedial courses that carry zero college credit. The consequences can be devastating: the National Center for Education Statistics reports only about 20 percent of U.S. students who take remedial reading or a combination of two nonreading remedial courses earn a bachelor's degree (Conley 2007).

A Systemwide Approach to Dual Enrollment

The history of Open Admissions at CUNY and the move to end remediation at its senior colleges have been well documented (Attewell and Lavin 2007; Parker 2007). Concomitant with the decision to move developmental coursework to the community colleges, the university set out to expand dual enrollment opportunities to all of New York City's public high school students by mandating that each of its seventeen undergraduate campuses offer dual enrollment. With policy and budgetary oversight from a Central Office administrative unit (see Kim, Chapter Six, in this volume), the CUNY College Now program expanded its enrollment from students in 110 high schools in 2000 to 249 high schools in 2005. Educational and administrative connections between the two largest urban public educational systems in the nation were fully underway.

Kingsborough Community College founded the College Now program in fall 1983, and by spring 1984 College Now offered its first courses to students in four large, comprehensive high schools in the borough of Brooklyn. At the time of systemwide expansion in fall 2000, CUNY's community colleges had been offering dual enrollment programming for two years. The start-up of the systemwide program initially involved the basic work of coming to a shared understanding of the definition of dual enrollment, but it took years to get all of the campuses to offer an adequate number of college credit courses to eligible high school students so that they could be counted as full participants in this CUNY-wide effort.

Program expansion across the largest urban public school system and the largest urban public university system meant becoming highly adept at managing complexity: College Now would connect the university's seventeen distinct two- and four-year colleges with hundreds of diverse high schools across New York City's five boroughs. Therefore, it became increasingly important for each campus to develop a stable of partner high schools. Within the partnership model, a high school could be partnered with a community college or a senior college (at CUNY, a senior college is a baccalaureate-granting college) depending on geographic proximity or high school theme, such as at small schools or career and technical education programs.

All CUNY colleges were charged and challenged to develop programming for high school students, many or most of whom would not enroll as freshmen at their college. If not the desired outcome for a given campus, this expectation did underscore the university's commitment to the public schools at a time when access to postsecondary education for underprepared students became the responsibility of the university's community colleges. Because College Now focuses on students *across* the system in ways that no other program at the university had done, it became clear that students would benefit if courses offered through one CUNY campus were honored at another. Programs and not students would be responsible for knowing if a course was transferable and how courses were counted at the receiving college so as to satisfy either general education or elective credits. If a course was unique to a campus and did not transfer, the sponsoring College Now program needed to make clear to students the immediate and subsequent value of the course. It became clear that a systemwide program amounted to more than the quality of each campus program; administrators needed to be aware of and account for college differences that could become unwelcome obstacles to the educational momentum students gained through program participation.

Expanding the Idea of Dual Enrollment

As administratively complex as the systemwide expansion of College Now turned out to be, the greater challenge emerged when program administrators began to identify and grapple with the educational tension inherent in expecting a dual enrollment program focused primarily on providing courses to "college-ready" students to mitigate the impact of ending remedial coursework at the baccalaureate-degree level, that is, to reduce significantly the number of students entering or failing remediation at CUNY.

Finding the moments inside individual high schools, and inside and between individual colleges, where students were falling off the college path—defined initially as eligibility for college credit course enrollment—became a College Now program priority and launched a whole set of qualitative and quantitative inquiries into the college readiness of students while in high school and then college. Seeing each student as dependent upon a program's ability to make the best of his or her participation in both that moment and going forward required a clear picture of a high school's and college's ability to prepare students for the challenges of college learning and college learning environments. Active and ongoing thinking about how a single program could serve students rooted in larger contexts became as much about identifying the challenges to student success as crafting programmatic and administrative responses—the hits and misses of program development.

The inquiry-based culture of the College Now program led to the expectation that program directors would learn to work with data on student participation and outcomes in the context of making the educational journey from high school to gaining a strong foothold in college (ideally, passing out of remediation upon entry) and that they would work closely with directors from other campuses in the interest of helping students manage the potential transition to another college. For example, program directors were expected to look at the demographics of their College Now student body as compared to the set of high schools with which they partnered and to citywide high school data. Within two years of expansion, it became clear that significant racial and gender disparities as measured by participation and successful course completion existed in all seventeen programs. To respond to enrollment data that revealed gaps in participation of black and Hispanic males, College Now program directors began to think carefully about their recruitment strategies and about building pathways into college readiness and college coursework for underprepared students.

Given that so many of the students in New York City's high schools do not meet the CUNY academic requirements for enrollment in college courses, prioritizing the recruitment of a representative student population alone would not lead to college course enrollment by a representative population as determined by race or ethnicity, gender, and by city borough. As a result of the comprehensive knowledge of the demographic, achievement, and graduation data of the city's schools, College Now launched a university-wide effort to build pathways into college awareness and preparation activities. This program development connected College Now to the biggest challenge faced by the university and responded directly to the original program mandate to expand dual enrollment opportunities for all the city's public high school students.

College Now's most creative effort to build a pathway for students ineligible for college credit course enrollment involved the development of Foundation Courses (Meade and Hofmann 2007). The majority of College Now precollege programming designed at the campuses to open up the program to underprepared students involved college-awareness activities, work that has yielded valuable contributions to national conversations about comprehensive dual enrollment programs (Hoffman 2005; Hooker and Brand 2009). But the Foundation Course development project raised the stakes on what dual enrollment programs could think about vis-à-vis students' academic needs. Developing courses that would address some of the important things experts do in a specific discipline drove the development of Foundation

Course curricula, which included selecting engaging disciplinary content as the context for helping students develop the skills necessary to be successful in discipline-specific courses. Some of the earliest curricular projects yielded "War and Technology," "Deciphering the Genetic Code," and "The Comic Spirit in Art and Literature."

An important principle for the development of Foundation Courses was that instructional design was always a collective endeavor; if the courses were not actually codesigned by disciplinary faculty, curriculum developers, and developmental educators, they were situated in a programmatic conversation about the needs of underprepared students making the transition from high school to CUNY colleges that have not, for the majority of incoming freshmen, demonstrated the educational advantages of their remedial pathways.

A program that by definition is offered to students while they are in high school, CUNY dual enrollment became an effective lens for understanding how any isolated activity, whether a college-credit course, a pre-college workshop, a Foundation Course, or a string of workshops or courses—even a three-week summer program—delivered in an administratively isolated way and without knowledge of the trajectory of a student's college-preparatory needs, would not lead to greater student achievement.

Dual Enrollment and CUNY's New Community College

Throughout the development of the concept for a new community college, it was important to be more inclusive of voices not typically charged with rethinking undergraduate education. The CUNY Chancellor turned to a unit within the university's Office of Academic Affairs responsible for helping students make the transition from high school to college. The director of the university's dual enrollment programs led a team that included educators from College Now, Adult Literacy and GED programs, adult and continuing education programs, and youth and early childhood development programs. Members of this team also included several senior staff from the New York City Department of Education's Career and Technical Education Office.

Part of working in dual enrollment at the system level involves developing the ability to support and strengthen relationships and interchange among multiple stakeholders in hundreds of high schools, the seventeen CUNY colleges, and the two large systems offices. Working with so many stakeholders, the Central Office College Now staff became skilled facilitators who were inclined to include professionals from the many dimensions of students' schooling, college transition, and college and community life in order to find the most effective ways to minimize institutional obstacles to student success. This program disposition for including many voices informed the process that was developed to produce the concept for a new college as well as the early stages of planning the new college. The planning team, as it came to be known, sought knowledge and experiences from our community college presidents, provosts, faculty, and staff; from a system-wide online survey; from a CUNY steering committee and an advisory board of distinguished educators and researchers; and from educators, researchers, and business people from New York City and across the nation.

The planning team reviewed the information gathered through con-sultation with hundreds of people and synthesized it into *A New Commu-nity College Concept Paper* (CUNY 2008). Discussing the entire structure of the college is beyond the scope of this chapter; however, there are impor-tant features of the new college that derive directly from the knowledge and practices of College Now.

Evidence-Based Program Design and Practice. A culture of inquiry supported by quantitative and qualitative research and evaluation informs pro-gram management and practice in College Now dual enrollment programs. The research and evaluation unit for these programs has helped program directors track students into and through CUNY and disaggregate data in order to help understand the impact of participation on different subgroups. A crucial development in understanding students across institutions was cre-ating a student matching algorithm; this algorithm enabled College Now to link participants from the program database to CUNY's data warehouse. Even-tually, the university would foster a data-sharing agreement with the New York City Department of Education to link high school and college data in order to better understand students' pathways through high school and into CUNY.

Developers of The New Community College emphasized asking ques-tions and collecting the data to understand CUNY's community college stu-dents. We collected extensive data on application and financial aid completion patterns, scores on CUNY entrance exams, course-taking patterns, the fre-quency with which students changed majors, and other information that helped paint a more complete profile of our students. As we met with col-leges to discuss initial findings, we were always surprised by how often administrators and faculty were making decisions based upon anecdotal evi-dence or what they perceived to be issues within the college. Later I discuss the reasons for requiring students to enroll full time at the New Commu-nity College during their first year, but as critics began to question the fea-sibility of requiring full-time enrollment, it was critical to explain that 90 percent of first-year students at CUNY already do attend full time.

Building upon this inquiry-driven approach, the Center for College Effectiveness at The New Community College of CUNY will combine tra-ditional institutional research and reporting with assessment of student learning, curricula, and professional development. Faculty and staff will work closely with the center to assess the college's educational practices and initiatives and to identify the instructional techniques, program content, and support services that best contribute to student success. Connecting institutional research with teaching and learning is a tricky matter, but using data to inform practice in order to improve student outcomes—when done collaboratively—can help guide the conversations that need to happen across traditionally separate areas of the college. The lessons of program management in College Now have demonstrated what can be done in this area.

Rethinking the Admissions Process. In 2004, the College Now program at Baruch College developed Think College Now, a twenty-hour workshop intended to provide early college and career awareness in order both to develop a pathway into college-credit courses as well as to provide students early support for understanding the steps they need to take to be successful in college. In *Redefining College Readiness*, Conley (2007, 27) notes that students need to know a great deal of information in order to "make good decisions about college preparation and to demystify the process . . . Activities to break [the application] process down into manageable pieces . . . will help increase the number of applicants and their subsequent success getting admitted to and succeeding in college." Think College Now and courses like it have been introduced across the College Now landscape and are helping students develop a stronger understanding of the college application process as well as the landscape of college and career choices.

Realizing that most New York City public high school students have not participated in college awareness activities like Think College Now, nor have they had access to intensive college advisement, The New Community College proposes an admission process that will perform a college preparatory function and help students develop and articulate an educational plan, as well as begin to create connections with the college's faculty and staff. In effect, admissions would serve as part of the transition to college. The authors of *Starting Right: A First Look at Engaging Entering Students* (Community College Survey of Student Engagement 2007, 7) explain that "At its best, the entry process offers opportunities to build relationships with students, help them set academic goals, bolster their commitment to attaining these goals, and provide critical academic advising and planning services."

As opposed to one-shot orientations that tend to be structured to serve the college-ready or self-reliant student, the new college will require information sessions as part of the admissions process. These sessions are meant to help impress upon students that open access should not amount to *uninformed* access. In part, the information sessions are designed to assess how much students know in light of how much they need to know about college and to explore with students the role community colleges can play in pursuit of a college degree and meaningful work. The information sessions will include faculty, staff, and peer mentors and be overseen by the director of college admissions and access, whose role it is to develop strong pathways into the college and ensure that students are provided with the knowledge they need early on to make an informed decision.

NEW DIRECTIONS FOR HIGHER EDUCATION • DOI:10.1002/he

Summer Programs and Full-Time Enrollment. The decisions to include a three-week summer bridge program and require full-time enrollment in the first year at The New Community College were informed, in part, by debates about whether students would attend newly designed four- to six-week, full-day College Now summer programs. College Now summer programs bring nearly 1,500 students to the CUNY campuses each year, and their advent was informed by a desire to provide students with sustained learning experiences. Discrete courses offered during the academic year are one way to reach students, but using the summer to immerse students in courses that are surrounded with support and noncredit activities seemed a logical next step in connecting students to college-going academic and cultural demands. The chorus of "No, high school students won't do that" was initially overwhelming but eventually wrong. Dual enrollment program staff became connoisseurs of statements about what high school students could not or would not do, and pushed forward with evidence of (and ideas to support) student learning.

The university expectation of expanding dual enrollment—initially defined as a singular college credit course—in order to mitigate the postsecondary challenges of underprepared high school students would prove to be limited and in need of ongoing revision. College Now summer programs provided the space to reimagine students' first academic experience on a college campus. New ideas like summer programs and a greater commitment by the colleges and students—along with our examination of emerging models across the country—led to a summer program for students at The New Community College: a required three-week, four-day summer bridge model designed to help students make a successful transition to the college and to begin to foster a sense of community and purpose.

Rethinking Developmental Education and the First Year. Even those students—especially community college students—who are able to navigate the application and matriculation process are often stymied by the educational and administrative structures intended to help them succeed academically and personally: "The separation of student services from classroom learning, the stratified approach to remediation outside the interesting work of disciplines, and the introductory course requirements across multiple departments create an environment of disconnect that works against student success . . . students often experience college, especially a commuter college, as a jigsaw puzzle of discrete courses, services, and administrative obligations" (CUNY 2008, 17). Similar to the way College Now leaders approached the development of Foundation Courses and other pathways and supports into and through college-level work, the New Community College sought to challenge the existing design of remedial and first-year college education. The first-year program at The New Community College provides an alternative to the programs at CUNY's six existing colleges and has some striking principles and features.

NEW DIRECTIONS FOR HIGHER EDUCATION • DOI:10.1002/he

The elimination of the long-established divide between developmental and college-level courses is one of the guiding principles of the New Community College. The first-year courses and student support structures integrate college preparatory skills, essential student services, and college-level content. The first-year program also introduces academic and practical learning about professions related to the majors.

The centerpiece of the first-year curriculum is the City Seminar, an interdisciplinary course that consists of four components. In the case study component, students will encounter an issue important to New York City and will explore the causes of the problem, the evolution of the problem over time, and possible solutions. The model will provide students with opportunities to engage with people and organizations connected to the topic through site and classroom visits, service learning, and other high-impact learning practices. The content addressed in case study is complemented by a quantitative reasoning component that strengthens students' mathematical skills, a reading and writing component that supports the literacy demands of the material, and a group workspace component that provides extra time to engage with the case study content and to practice literacy and numeracy skills.

Students will enroll in Ethnographies of Work during the first year, a course that introduces them to the role and meaning of work in society and to individuals. Ethnographies also introduces academic and practical learning about professions related to the programs of study so that students may begin making informed choices regarding a major. The first year will also include a statistics course and English composition.

All students will attend college full time, at least for the first year. "The full-time requirement is shaped by the belief that unprepared students require more sustained time to develop, practice, and demonstrate *beyond the level of minimum proficiency* the skills and knowledge they will need for associate degree completion, baccalaureate transfer, and/or workplace readiness" (CUNY 2008, 7–8). The additional hours and the deeply connected work, together with a highly structured cohort model of teaching and learning, will provide our typically underprepared first-time community college students with a program of study that will build their academic confidence and independence.

Conclusion

Thinking about prepared, underprepared, and underrepresented students—and thinking about their schools and colleges, and running dual enrollment missions between those schools and colleges for years and years—has led to significant educational experiences that are much larger than offering a single college credit course to a high school student or, specifically, offering 28,000 enrollments to 20,000 high school students across New York City.

The important learning opportunities for the professional who manages or teaches in CUNY's College Now program have been and continue to be meaningful to the stepped-up efforts across the nation to improve student learning, retention, and graduation.

References

Attewell, P., and D. Lavin. 2007. *Passing the Torch: Does Higher Education for the Disadvantaged Pay Off Across the Generations*. New York: Russell Sage Foundation Publications.

City University of New York (CUNY). 2008. *A New Community College Concept Paper*. New York: City University of New York.

Community College Survey of Student Engagement. 2007. *Starting Right: A First Look at Engaging Entering Students*. Austin, TX: Community College Survey of Student Engagement.

Conley, D. 2007. *Redefining College Readiness, Volume 3*. Eugene, OR: Educational Policy Improvement Center.

Hoffman, N. 2005. *Add and Subtract: Dual Enrollment as a State Strategy to Increase Postsecondary Success for Underrepresented Students*. Double the Numbers: A Jobs for the Future Initiative. Boston: Jobs for the Future.

Hooker, S., and B. Brand. 2009. *Success at Every Step: How 23 Programs Support Youth on the Path to College and Beyond*. Washington, DC: American Youth Policy Forum.

Meade, T., and E. Hofmann. 2007. "CUNY College Now: Extending the Reach of Dual Enrollment." In *Minding the Gap*, edited by N. Hoffman, J. Vargas, A. Venezia, and M. Miller. Cambridge, MA: Harvard University Press.

Parker, T. L. 2007. *Ending College Remediation: Consequences for Access and Opportunity*. ASHE/Lumina Policy Brief and Critical Essays no. 2. Ames: Department of Educational Leadership and Policy Studies, Iowa State University.

Santos, F. 2011. "College Readiness Is Lacking, City Reports Show." *New York Times* Oct. 24.

TRACY MEADE *is director of strategic planning and program development in the Office of Academic Affairs at The City University of New York. Previously she was director of CUNY's New Community College Initiative.*

New Directions for Higher Education • DOI:10.1002/he

11

This chapter addresses some of the tensions inherent to dual enrollment and relates them to larger challenges in higher education.

Dual Enrollment as a Liminal Space

Eric Hofmann, Daniel Voloch

In early spring 2010, a student sent an e-mail to the general mailbox of College Now, The City University of New York's (CUNY) comprehensive dual enrollment program. The subject line read, "colleges associated with the program." The questioner identified herself as "julia" and sent the following message at 11:23 p.m.: "I am planning to attend an ivy specifically harvard. Does this program have the courses that harvard has?"

Julia's e-mail highlights the extraordinary position of dual enrollment as a place between high school and college that is neither exclusively one nor the other. Dual enrollment inhabits a space where larger questions about higher education—the cultural practices, norms, institutional relationships and interactions, and the overall "business" of learning—are grappled with on a daily basis. To the metaphors around college transition, such as the "gap" (Hoffman et al. 2007) or "continuum" (Conley 2010), we add another: the liminal space. Unlike the clearly-articulated path of a continuum or the simple bridging of a gap, dual enrollment as a "liminal space" conveys the concomitant unease of dissolved boundaries and creates a productive tension that requires secondary and postsecondary institutions to articulate together their expectations for "college-ready students" and "college-level work."

The Tensions in Dual Enrollment

When CUNY ended open admissions at its senior colleges in 1999 and aligned entrance to its baccalaureate programs with specific scores on the New York State high school exams, the university moved all its colleges to implement dual enrollment (Badillo 1999). CUNY expanded College Now systemwide as a purposeful college transition strategy, one that over time has focused predominantly on serving students in the academic midrange.

New Directions for Higher Education, no. 158, Summer 2012 © Wiley Periodicals, Inc.
Published online in Wiley Online Library (wileyonlinelibrary.com) • DOI:10.1002/he.20019

With the mission to help students graduate from high school prepared to do college-level work, the program, like many others described in this volume, is a departure from the traditional dual enrollment focus on providing college-level "enrichment" opportunities for advanced students.

CUNY's community colleges were first on board in the expansion, as several already had versions of dual enrollment and a few strong partnerships with nearby feeder schools. After two years, each of the seventeen undergraduate campuses had some type of program in place; however, the challenges then and over the following years highlighted key areas of questions about the nature of college-level learning, institutional identity, and K–12 and higher education policy. We describe a few of the tensions dual enrollment has exposed here at CUNY and, by all accounts, at institutions across the country.

The first set of issues revolves around the questions of what constitutes college-level work, who is responsible for preparing students, and which students are ready to complete this type of work. Additional questions relate to the various goals of dual enrollment vis-à-vis multiple stakeholders, such as college administrators, policy makers, and parents and students.

High School Students and College-Level Learning. In this volume, Hughes and Edwards as well as Klopfenstein and Lively address the recent move to expand dual enrollment opportunities to a wider range of students, including those who may be academically at risk or may not have met traditional benchmarks of college readiness. Yet even when high school students meet academic requirements, as is the case with most dual enrollment programs, concerns continue to surface as to participants' maturity and ability to handle more rigorous assignments, or even the rationale for accelerating learning in the first place. Pushback is common (see, for example, Rosenbach and Katopes 2010).

The complaint that high school students are not capable of college study or that this level of study is not intended for them raises the question of defining college-level learning, especially in the area of general education, a difficult task within the context of diverse disciplines and academic departments, institutional variation, and faculty prerogatives. On the postsecondary level, the Liberal Education and America's Promise (LEAP) initiative from the Association of American Colleges and Universities emphasizes the need for explicit learning outcomes and rubrics, intentional course sequencing, and authentic assessments (http://www.aacu.org/leap/). At the front end of readiness is the move toward the Common Core State Standards Initiative (2011) that addresses college-level competencies for college readiness along a K–12 trajectory. Dual enrollment is a nexus between these initiatives, a space that can help educators across sectors better understand and articulate the value of postsecondary learning broadly and liberal arts learning more specifically.

In an analysis of the role that dual enrollment can play in developing or refining learning standards, Hoffman (2007) writes that "alignment of standards, assessments, and curriculum across the divide in order to lower college remediation and drop-out rates is generally disconnected from dual enrollment, but making this connection could contribute to a new conception of how to make the border between high school and college more permeable (rather than better policed)" (198). One of the most important issues facing postsecondary institutions is the ability to provide effective developmental education that allows students to enroll in college courses. Similarly, one of the most important issues facing high schools is identifying key competencies for college readiness and developing curricula and programming to ensure that students graduate from high school prepared to enroll and succeed in college. Working together in the liminal space of dual enrollment, high schools and colleges can create programs that not only better prepare students for postsecondary success by introducing them to the language, rigor, and skills necessary to complete college credit work, but also allow both institutions to develop clearly-articulated benchmarks and standards.

A related question asks what constitutes college-level pedagogy and student performance. A persistent assumption throughout postsecondary institutions is that what takes place in a college classroom for college credit denotes college-level work. But what actually happens in the classroom? A recent study (Arum and Roksa 2011) uses data from the College Learning Assessment (CLA) to suggest that a majority of students in the sample made no significant gains in learning in their first years of college. Whether this is an accurate reflection of something as complex as learning, the study raises interesting questions about how we assess learning and link outcomes with specific content or teaching practices. Embracing the liminal space created by dual enrollment challenges the assumption that college is defined by who is in the classroom—a member of the faculty and "college" students—and raises important questions, such as: What should college teaching look like? Is it a matter of simply removing all scaffolding? What defines rigor in a college classroom? How much, and what kind, of content must be covered?

The question of which courses to offer through dual enrollment is also significant, and it relates to a program's mission. Are dual enrollment courses intended to provide academically strong students with an opportunity to take courses that are not offered in their high schools, as described by Kinnick (Chapter Five) or Klopfenstein and Lively (Chapter Seven) in this volume? Highlight the strengths of the participating college and raise the profile of community colleges? Develop pathways into college credit courses for students who may not be ready? Or should dual enrollment provide scaffolded practice with rigorous readings and assignments in order to allow high school students to anticipate and enact, as Karp has described in this volume, the role of college students? The answers to these questions should influence course offerings. Dual enrollment programs, as well as the higher education institutions that support them, need to define their goals clearly and ensure the coursework aligns with those goals.

High School and the Higher Education Mission. Like the criticisms described in the previous section, the argument that high schools are not part of the higher education mission hinges on maintaining the borders of institutions, as if preparation—and learning on the whole—were a fixed characteristic, or, within Conley's (2010) formulation, a "cut point and not a continuum." In this environment, dual enrollment programs are the point of first encounter for issues pertaining to college access. But the history of the public university—the CUNYs and their cousins—is richly linked to the public schools, and many institutions continue to be connected through teacher education programs and a common student body.

As indicated throughout this volume, many educators and policy makers believe that dual enrollment participation can promote college access and success, a possibility suggested by Adelman (1999) in the initial *Toolbox* study. At CUNY, some campus academic departments choose not to offer dual enrollment courses, and constituents across the university have questioned the value of using increasingly scarce resources to enrich the education of students who may ultimately enroll elsewhere. In Chapter Five, Kinnick describes the Dual Enrollment Honors Program (DEHP) at Kennesaw State University and demonstrates the value one program adds to its institution. At the same time, the high academic profile of those participants underscores a suggestion by Morest and Karp (2007) that maintaining the highest admissions standards for dual enrollment programs could exclude those students who might benefit most from the experience.

The mission question is particularly thorny for community college faculty and administrators, as it is linked to the place of these institutions in higher education, a situation that Grubb and Worthen (1999) have referred to as "the special dilemmas of community college." We have encountered community college faculty and administrators who feel that their institutions are fighting for respect from their colleagues in more selective institutions, and who fear that participating in dual enrollment programs only reinforces their perceived status as glorified high school teachers. For faculty who see their allegiance more towards their discipline than towards their students, working with high schools undermines their own professional identity and might be seen as diminishing their work. Turning to Hughes and Edwards in this volume, however, we should recognize the power that comes from having college faculty engage with high school students in a structured program built around student success.

Recruitment versus Access and Success. Although dual enrollment should be considered an important recruitment tool for the institution—an opportunity to showcase the best of the college—we cannot overlook the broader goal of school–college partnerships in the conversation around college access and success. Dual enrollment programs give students a view of opportunities beyond high school, especially for students facing socioeconomic roadblocks to success. CUNY College Now has heard from scores of students for whom dual enrollment played an important role in their success, such as a student in the Bronx who was first in her family to go to college and eventually received a Gates Millennium scholarship. She credits the community college library where she participated in College Now as a place of safety and quiet where she could concentrate on her schoolwork (N. Camara, personal communication with Daniel Voloch, December 2011). Or the student who enrolled in several dual enrollment courses at CUNY's Lehman College and made his way upstate to a residential college, where the dormitory provided some of the physical comforts that eluded him in his home (Joseph 2011).

Even as these students left the CUNY system after participating in dual enrollment, the university has reaped the overall benefits of program participation. In fall 2010, 29.1 percent of public high school graduates entering CUNY as first-time freshmen had College Now experience. Also worth noting is the percentage of New York City public school graduates entering CUNY within three months of graduating in 2008: 44.3 percent of College Now participants versus 29.4 percent of those who did not participate in the program. When we look at students who entered within fifteen months of their 2008 high school graduation, we see College Now participants' enrollment in CUNY jumps to 51.9 percent. Furthermore, the majority of College Now students who participated through our community colleges and matriculated at CUNY enrolled in a senior college.

Education in the U.S.: A Tiered System. The U.S. higher education system is vast, and perceptions of quality and purpose permeate conversations across the school–college divide. These conversations play out at the local level for student advocates. For example, staff in CUNY's College Now program have fielded countless requests from schools to partner with senior colleges rather than community colleges because they believe the dual enrollment experience at a four-year college is more valuable for their students. Our response that most courses are transferrable at least in CUNY has been bolstered by the university's current move toward a more aligned general education core and, therefore, easier articulation for students who transfer among the seventeen campuses.

Although transfer within the system is an important issue to address, transfer of dual enrollment credits outside the system is something that would not be familiar to the typical high school student. According to Adelman (1999), 60 percent of undergraduates will attend more than one institution and 40 percent will transfer across state lines. Julia's e-mail that opened this chapter reveals a level of understanding around this issue that is uncommon for the typical high school student: Does College Now have the classes Harvard has? Will Harvard accept credits from a CUNY college? These are bigger questions that go beyond the scope of dual enrollment but crystallize the issues for the student as stakeholder.

With all the effort to make students college-ready, it is incumbent on higher education to learn how to make their institutions "student-ready"

(Garvey 2009). Dual enrollment is a powerful liminal space that influences colleges to develop a better understanding of their students' needs and habits before they arrive and to develop partnerships that will serve as levers for educational renewal or, in the examples highlighted by both Edmunds (Chapter Nine) and Meade (Chapter Ten) in this volume, that can create new educational structures.

Conclusion

Dual enrollment program staff—in many cases, neither strictly faculty nor administrators—play an important role in defining the liminal space their programs inhabit. These practitioners collaborate, advocate, counsel, and advise, all while navigating the shifting landscapes of schools and colleges and responding to the requests of academic departments and admissions offices and the needs of participating students. It is critical to bring their voices to discussions around postsecondary transition and the characteristics of college-ready students and student-ready colleges.

Collectively, the chapters in this volume have hinted at the tensions that surround these programs, including questions about the ability (or even desirability) of high school students to complete college-level work, the characteristics of "college-level" study and pedagogy, the civic responsibility of postsecondary institutions and their role within broader educational reform measures, and the benchmarks used to measure success across programs and institutions. We argue that the resolution of these tensions is not the goal. Instead, we hope that institutions across the K–16 landscape embrace the opportunity for school–college collaboration as a means of developing stronger pathways and helping students and practitioners better understand the skills, knowledge, and experiences necessary to succeed in college.

References

Adelman, C. 1999. *Answers in the Tool Box: Academic Intensity, Attendance Patterns, and Bachelor's Degree Attainment*. Washington, DC: U.S. Department of Education.

Arum, R., and J. Roksa. 2011. *Academically Adrift: Limited Learning on College Campuses*. Chicago: University of Chicago Press.

Badillo, H. 1999. "A Message from the Chairman of the CUNY Board of Trustees." *CUNY Matters* Summer.

Common Core State Standards Initiative. 2011. Accessed January 2, 2012, from http://www.corestandards.org/.

Conley, D. T. 2010. "Replacing Remediation with Readiness." Paper presented at National Center for Postsecondary Research Developmental Education Conference, New York, September.

Garvey, J. 2009. *Are New York City's Public Schools Preparing Students for Success in College?* Providence, RI: Annenberg Institute for School Reform.

Grubb, W. N., and H. Worthen. 1999. *Honored But Invisible: An Inside Look at Teaching in Community Colleges*. New York: Routledge.

Hoffman, N. 2007. "Using Dual Enrollment to Build a 9-14 System." In *Minding the Gap*, edited by N. Hoffman, J. Vargas, A. Venezia, and M. S. Miller. Cambridge, MA: Harvard Education Press.

Hoffman, N., J. Vargas, A. Venezia, and M. S. Miller, Eds. 2007. *Minding the Gap*. Cambridge, MA: Harvard Education Press.

Joseph, C. 2011. "From a Cold Apartment to a Utica College Dorm Room." *New York Times* Dec. 4: A35.

Morest, V. S., and M. M. Karp. 2007. "Twice the Credit, Half the Time? The Growth of Dual Credit at Community Colleges and High School." In *Defending the Community College Agenda*, edited by T. Bailey and V. S. Morest. Baltimore: The Johns Hopkins University Press.

Rosenbach, N., and P. Katopes. 2010. "The Lesson of Delicate Arch." *Inside Higher Ed.* Accessed December 1, 2011, from http://www.insidehighered.com/views/2010/05/04/arch.

ERIC HOFMANN *is university director for Collaborative Programs at The City University of New York.*

DANIEL VOLOCH *is director of CUNY At Home in College. Previously he was director of the College Now dual enrollment program at Hostos Community College.*

INDEX

ORDER FORM SUBSCRIPTION AND SINGLE ISSUES

DISCOUNTED BACK ISSUES:

Use this form to receive 20% off all back issues of *New Directions for Higher Education*.
All single issues priced at **$23.20** (normally $29.00)

TITLE	ISSUE NO.	ISBN

Call 888-378-2537 or see mailing instructions below. When calling, mention the promotional code JBNND to receive your discount. For a complete list of issues, please visit www.josseybass.com/go/ndhe

SUBSCRIPTIONS: (1 YEAR, 4 ISSUES)

☐ New Order ☐ Renewal

U.S.	☐ Individual: $89 ☐ Institutional: $275
CANADA/MEXICO	☐ Individual: $89 ☐ Institutional: $315
ALL OTHERS	☐ Individual: $113 ☐ Institutional: $349

Call 888-378-2537 or see mailing and pricing instructions below.
Online subscriptions are available at www.onlinelibrary.wiley.com

ORDER TOTALS:

Issue / Subscription Amount: $ _____

Shipping Amount: $ _____
(for single issues only – subscription prices include shipping)

Total Amount: $ _____

SHIPPING CHARGES:

First Item	$6.00
Each Add'l Item	$2.00

(No sales tax for U.S. subscriptions. Canadian residents, add GST for subscription orders. Individual rate subscriptions must be paid by personal check or credit card. Individual rate subscriptions may not be resold as library copies.)

BILLING & SHIPPING INFORMATION:

☐ **PAYMENT ENCLOSED:** *(U.S. check or money order only. All payments must be in U.S. dollars.)*

☐ **CREDIT CARD:** ☐ VISA ☐ MC ☐ AMEX

Card number _____ Exp. Date _____

Card Holder Name _____ Card Issue # _____

Signature _____ Day Phone _____

☐ **BILL ME:** *(U.S. institutional orders only. Purchase order required.)*

Purchase order # _____
Federal Tax ID 13559302 • GST 89102-8052

Name _____

Address _____

Phone _____ E-mail _____

Copy or detach page and send to: **John Wiley & Sons, One Montgomery Street, Suite 1200, San Francisco, CA 94104-4594**

Order Form can also be faxed to: **888-481-2665**

PROMO JBNND